WHAT PEOPLE ARE SAYING ABOUT *IMMEDIATE OBEDIENCE . . .*

"And they straightway left their nets, and followed him" (Matt. 4:19, KJV). I relish and cherish Rod Loy's book as a skillful meditation on the significance of that word *straightway*, and an exciting unveiling of a theology of obedience. Read this book to find out why the secret of a vitalizing relationship with God is hidden in the etymology of that word *obedience*, which comes from the Latin verb "obediere" v   means "to hear into heeding."

Leonard Sweet
Best-selling author, professor (Drew University, George Fox University), and chief contributor to sermons.com

This is the sort of book that should be read by every followe Jesus. With personal vulnerability and strong biblical teaching, Rod l directs minds and hearts to the wonder of having a powerful and personal relationship with the living God. No one will read this book and come away untouched. Rod's message of listening and responding to God convicts us—because we all fall short—and inspires us—because we long for this kind of connection with God. The concluding 90-Day Challenge provides clear and accessible guidelines as to how to relate one's faith to immediate obedience.

Robert E. Cooley
President Emeritus, Gordon-Conwell Theological Seminary

Rod Loy has done it again—provided a practical, no-nonsense approach to living out the Christian life. In *Immediate Obedience*, Pastor Rod removes the mystery surrounding obeying God and challenges us to join him in the adventure of immediately acting on the small prompts God gives us every day. Get ready to grow!

Donna Hill
Vice President of Student Affairs, College of the Ouachitas

Rod has unlocked some practical and challenging insights that are essential for every Christ follower! He walks the reader through practical ways of learning to hear God's voice and the importance of saying yes immediately. This book has challenged me to listen and obey on a daily basis. I want to be in a position for God to use me in every arena of my life, and Rod in *Immediate Obedience* has helped me get there! Great book—a must read!

John McKinzie
Lead Pastor, Hope Fellowship Church, Frisco, TX

Rod Loy is an incredibly insightful writer. He stirs your intellect . . . grips your imagination . . . empowers your resolve . . . excites your emotions. You, the reader, are drawn into his understanding. The game is changed when you read what Rod writes. So, enrich yourself as you explore Rod's thought processes in this book. The mundane will vanish as you dismember "delayed obedience" from your usual response to truth. Read on and admit it: it's time for a transformation. Priceless!

J. Don George
Founding Pastor, Calvary Church, Irving, Texas

God has not merely called us to action. He has called us to obedience. In his book, *Immediate Obedience,* Pastor Rod Loy captures the essence of what it means to be obedient to God, not just with our church life but with every moment of every ordinary day. Grounded in Scripture and illustrated beautifully with stories from Rod's personal journey of immediate obedience, this book will challenge both the new believer and the veteran minister of the gospel. Rod brings a new depth of understanding to the concept of being obedient to God. Reading our Bible, praying over our meals, and going to church are not enough to please God with our obedience. Obedience requires sensitivity to God's voice, compassion for others, generosity, immediacy, and discipline. I plan to challenge every person in my church to read this book and break the habits of disobedience in their own lives.

David M. Wigington
Lead Pastor, Cornerstone Christian Fellowship

Rod Loy has acute spiritual insight. In his new book, he cuts through the haze of spiritual concepts and captures the heart of a relationship with God: listening to His voice and responding in obedience. No excuses, no delays. Rod's message is the most freeing and challenging one I've ever heard!

Dr. George O. Wood
General Superintendent of the Assemblies of God

Immediate obedience. It sounds like a challenge, and it is. In Rod Loy's book, he outlines the essence of a life of faith. It's not enough to go through the motions and look like a good Christian. True spiritual life is a vital connection with the God of the universe and a heart to obey Him—no matter what the consequences and whatever the blessings God gives. Rod's insights thrill me and terrify me . . . which I imagine is how Jesus' disciples felt every day.

Dr. Alton Garrison
Assistant General Superintendent of the Assemblies of God

I recommend *Immediate Obedience* to every believer. There are hundreds of good books out there, but few writers and teachers have the pulse of God's heart like Rod Loy. He invites us to listen to God's shouts and whispers, and he challenges us to obey whatever God tells us to do. Buckle up when you read it. It'll blow you away!

Bryan Koch
Lead Pastor, Glad Tidings Church, Reading, PA

The essence of following Christ is obedience, yet there is a huge chasm between knowing that truth and effectively living it out in everyday life. That's why I am so excited by the message of *Immediate Obedience*. Drawing from firsthand experience and a fresh perspective from Scripture, Rod Loy shares valuable lessons for those of us desiring to be disciples on whom God can depend.

Dr. Kermit Bridges
President, Southwestern Assemblies of God University

I've had a front row seat for Rod's adventure of obedience. He's not just writing about it, he's living it! Pastors, this principle in action will change your church. But, the principle works for more than just pastors.

Business leaders, stay-at-home moms and dads and students will all benefit for listening for God's voice and immediately obeying. Take the challenge. You'll never be the same.

Larry Moore
District Superintendent of the Arkansas Assemblies of God

No matter who you are, you will find yourself in Pastor Rod's book. The simple and daring Christian discipline of immediate obedience is a truth presented in a way that will convict, challenge, and give you hope.

Imagine a world where people say yes to Jesus before they know the question. It would be a world with less hunger, less poverty, less pain, and most important of all, less spiritual darkness. If all Pentecostal believers would anticipate the Holy Spirit's voice and be immediately obedient, we would change our world. When called to tribes hostile to the gospel, to the last reached, to the dangerous places, we would not stop to count the cost. The cost would not matter. We would simply find a way to go and tell them about Jesus.

I wonder who is depending on me to practice immediate obedience. Who needs me to ease their pain? Who needs me to help them make it through their day? And the most haunting question of all: Will they be eternally lost if I don't?

Greg Beggs
Africa Regional Director, Assemblies of God World Missions

Rod Loy doesn't just stand back and instruct people to follow Jesus. He lets us know he's down in the trenches with us. In *Immediate Obedience*, he shares the joy of seeing God work in and through him as he learns to respond to God's voice, but he is also bluntly honest about his struggles and failures. We need someone like Rod to show us the way, someone who combines lofty hope with realistic patience. His book will inspire you like nothing you've ever read before.

Dary Northrup
Senior Pastor, Timberline Church, Fort Collins, CO

God never intended life to be boring. His plan is to use each and every person in their context to be strategic partners with Him in touching lives. Rod Loy challenges each one of us to a life of significance and adventure as we listen and obey. It isn't something that only occurs for spiritual giants. It is possible for everyone if we will only take the time to listen and obey. I loved the book! It challenged me to tune my heart moment by moment to God's direction so that I can be used by Him whenever, wherever.

Scott Hanson
Strategic Leader — Unreached People Groups in Africa,
Assemblies of God World Missions

Inspiring . . . motivating . . . challenging . . . and practical! Rod's personal journey and insight moves me to listen better to God's heart so I can be His hands. Every believer needs to read this book to learn how to listen and obey—so simple and yet so difficult!

Pastor Darius Johnston
Lead Pastor, Christ Church Fort Worth, Fort Worth, TX

Rod gives us a perfect definition of what success looks like in the kingdom of God: immediate obedience. All of us who are serious about living for Jesus want to be successful in being His disciple, but don't always know how to do it. Rod gives us practical insights on how to live "naturally supernatural" in our everyday life. This book could literally change your life.

Scott Wilson
Senior Pastor, The Oaks Fellowship, Dallas, TX

Oswald Chambers once said, "All God's revelations are sealed for us until they are opened to us by obedience." In this inspired book, *Immediate Obedience*, Rod Loy presents anew the tremendous benefits of prompt obedience to God by sharing personal experiences, illustrations, and a biblical perspective. The book also sparked a childhood memory—and I am not sure who coined this phrase, but my mother used to say, "The key to deliverance is instant obedience." Many biblical examples and my own life experiences substantiate this truth. Thank you, Rod, for this book, a gift to the Christian community that reignites our heart's desire to obey the Lord immediately.

Dr. Greg Mundis
Executive Director, Assemblies of God World Missions

Rod nails it with *Immediate Obedience* and helps make something so supernatural, feel so normal and so user friendly. Too many Christians struggle with hearing and obeying God and *Immediate Obedience* will bring clarity and direction to these areas. Read it right away, study it, and make it part of your life. *Immediate Obedience* is the tool you need to help clarify the voice of God and the prompts we all should obey!

Rob Ketterling
Lead Pastor , River Valley Church, Apple Valley, MN

IMMEDIATE

OBEDIENCE

THE ADVENTURE OF TUNING IN TO GOD

ROD LOY

Published by Influence Resources
1445 N. Boonville Ave.
Springfield, Missouri 65802

Cover design by Sheepish Designs
Interior formatting by Anne McLaughlin

Note: In some of the stories in this book, the names and details have been changed to protect anonymity.

ISBN: 978-1-62912-109-3
17 16 15 14 • 1 2 3 4 5

Printed in the United States of America

This book is dedicated to my wife, Cindy, and to my church family at First Assembly of God in North Little Rock, Arkansas.

It was Cindy who first challenged me to write this book. She is making the obedience journey with me. It's awesome to have a life partner who is committed to obey God without questioning the cost!

Hundreds of people at First NLR took the "immediate obedience" challenge. Their stories are exciting and their experience is life changing. To all of you, thank you for putting your obedience into action and sharing your stories. I love you, and I'm so proud of you. I can't wait to see how God uses your continuing obedience!

CONTENTS

ACKNOWLEDGEMENTS

Thanks to my sons, Tyler and Parker, for allowing me to share countless stories from your lives. I'm super proud of your willingness to obey God without hesitation.

I'm grateful to my friend, Pat Springle, who once again helped me put principles and stories on paper. Your heart and passion is a gift to the church and to me!

Finally, thank you to the staff, campus pastors, and board of First NLR, for making space for me to write, dream, and to share what God puts on my heart. There's no team I'd rather share life with.

INTRODUCTION:
WHO'S LISTENING?

*"Prayer is not monologue, but dialogue; God's voice is its most
essential part. Listening to God's voice is the secret of the assurance
that He will listen to mine."*
—Andrew Murray

Busy, tired, and confused. That's an accurate description of many people in our culture—including many Christians. As we react to the external demands we face each day, it's all we can do to keep up with our priorities—and to be honest, we often choose the wrong things to put at the top of our lists. We're incredibly busy, and everything seems equally urgent. At the end of the day we're exhausted, yet we wonder if we accomplished anything meaningful at all.

As Christians, we want to stand before Jesus someday and hear Him say, "Well done, good and faithful servant! . . . Come and share your master's happiness!" (Matt. 25:21) But many of us live with a secret, nagging doubt. We wonder if our choices please Him, and we're not sure our lives are making a difference.

There's another way—a better way to live, a better way to connect to God, and a better way to be assured that our lives matter. It's by making a commitment to obey God immediately, no matter what He tells us to

> Every moment (no matter how ordinary) might be a "God moment," and every encounter with someone (no matter how annoying) might be a "divine appointment."

do. When we respond in active faith as soon as we hear His voice, everything changes! We become more in tune with the heart of God and more sensitive to the people around us, and we get a front row seat to watch God do incredible things in us and through us. We experience the abundant life Christ promised to those who truly follow Him.

When we learn to capture each moment, we live with a sense of expectant wonder. Every moment (no matter how ordinary) might be a "God moment," and every encounter with someone (no matter how annoying) might be a "divine appointment." Our priority shifts from accomplishing our selfish agendas to fulfilling God's kingdom agenda.

A YEAR, A LIFETIME

People who know me say I'm a pretty disciplined and detailed guy. I think it's the product of both nature and nurture. My father was a computer programmer and trouble-shooter for IBM. I have his genes, and I saw how he handled goals and problems.

Many years ago I developed the habit of setting goals in six different areas of my life at the beginning of every year—not just one goal, but several goals for each of the six areas. Then I created a detailed plan to fit them all into my schedule. However, by the third or fourth month of each year, the mass and complexity of all those goals proved to be overwhelming . . . even for someone who is naturally disciplined and focused. After several years of frustration, I decided to narrow the next year's goals to one in each of the six areas. Even that proved to be too many, so I pared my focus down to just one goal that would be my focus for the entire year.

I asked myself, "What's the one area of my life that, if I grow and change, will make me a better person and a better leader?" To narrow the range of options (and there are always many), I used three filters: prayer, self-awareness, and the input of others who know me well. I asked God to put one thing on my heart. I knew He could show me a million things in my life that needed improvement, but I asked Him to target just one for the year. I trusted Him to give me a big, clear mirror of truth so I could see what I do well and what areas needed work. Human beings have an almost limitless capacity for self-deception, so I don't take self-analysis lightly. As I prayed and thought, I asked my wife Cindy and a few good friends to give me feedback about what they saw in my life. I chose people who are perceptive, had my best interests at heart, and most importantly, had the courage to tell me the truth.

When I went through this process a few years ago, God put "quick forgiveness" on my heart. I didn't tell our church about it, and I didn't lead any campaigns to teach it. I realized that if it didn't first sink deeply into my own experience, I didn't have any business telling others to do it. For a year, I asked myself, *Do I forgive others the way God forgives me?*

In the Lord's Prayer, Jesus taught us to pray, "Forgive us our debts, as we also have forgiven our debtors" (Matt. 6:12). That doesn't mean

God's forgiveness is conditional, based on our willingness to forgive. It's just the opposite. Our willingness and capacity to forgive those who hurt us is an overflow of our experience of Christ's complete, full, and instantaneous forgiveness of our sins. Paul picks up this connection in two of his letters when he explains, "Be kind and compassionate to one another, forgiving each other, just as in Christ God forgave you" (Eph. 4:32, cf. Col. 3:13).

Every day that year, I asked God to drive the power and beauty of forgiveness deeper into my heart until it spilled out into my relationships. Of course, when trying to forgive someone who has hurt or betrayed us, we experience the natural barrier of resentment. As I prayed, God reminded me of certain people I had excused and tried to forget, but hadn't really forgiven. It was a wonderful, cleansing year that drove me deeper into the heart of God and the gospel of grace. When the year ended, I was finally ready to share my experiences with others.

Another year, God put it on my heart to focus on "immediate obedience." At first, I wasn't sure what that meant. Wasn't I already obeying God? I thought responding to God's whispers, nudges, impressions, and shouts was a strength in my walk with Him. As I prayed and read the Scriptures, however, the Lord showed me some gaps—some big gaps—in my responsiveness to Him. I was responding, but sometimes slowly or even reluctantly. So every morning as I recited, "Your kingdom come, Your will be done on earth as it is in heaven," my additional prayer was, "God, let me hear Your voice and sense Your leading so that I *immediately* obey You."

I didn't want to miss any "God moments" because of spiritual deafness or delayed responses. I asked God to clean out my spiritual ears, give me a receptive and sensitive heart, and provide the courage to act instantly on whatever He told me to do.

This was to be "the year of immediate obedience." My first act of obedience was to accept God's directive to make this commitment for the year. He had spoken, and it was up to me to instantly obey. I had no idea where all this was going, but I signed on for the ride. I felt a lot of uncertainty—and honestly, genuine fear. I also felt a little confused. After all, I was the pastor of a church. I shouldn't feel threatened by God's invitation to hear His voice and respond in faith, but I quickly realized this commitment opened new doors of spiritual experience. What would He ask me to do? Would I be embarrassed when I obeyed Him? Would I *look* weird? Would I *be* weird?

Every morning for a year, I asked God to make me sensitive to His voice so that I would take action and make His kingdom come more fully to the people I meet each day. I thought of the old song that says,

"I'll go where you want me to go, dear Lord,

Over mountain or plain or sea;

I'll say what you want me to say, dear Lord;

I'll be what you want me to be."[1]

THE ATTITUDE OF JESUS

Throughout the year, God kept reminding me of a passage in Paul's letter to the Philippians. He wrote, "Do nothing out of selfish ambition or vain conceit. Rather, in humility value others above yourselves, not looking to your own interests but each of you to the interests of the others. In your relationships with one another, have the same mindset as Christ Jesus" (Phil. 2:3–5).

Have the same attitude as Christ—what in the world was Paul talking about? Is that even possible? The apostle doesn't leave us guessing. He says that Christ's attitude was complete surrender to the will of the Father: "He humbled himself and became obedient to death—even death on a cross!" (Phil. 2:8)

In the classic devotional, *My Utmost for His Highest*, Oswald Chambers encourages us to listen to God no matter what He says to us:

> "Get into the habit of saying, 'Speak, Lord,' and life will become a romance. Every time circumstances press in on you say, 'Speak, Lord,' and make time to listen. Chastening is more than a means of discipline—it is meant to bring me to the point of saying, 'Speak, Lord.' Think back to a time when God spoke to you. Do you remember what he said? As we listen, our ears become more sensitive, and like Jesus, we will hear God all the time."[2]

One morning as I thought and prayed through the passage in Philippians, I realized, I wasn't yet at that point. I concluded that I was *fairly* obedient to God. If someone put a gun to my head and threatened to kill me if I said I was a follower of Christ, I think I would have the courage to claim to know Him. But this was different. God was asking me to be so obedient that I was willing to die to my own agenda, schedule, and desires—not just once, but all day every day.

Plenty of people say they're willing to die for Christ, but if you don't live a life of obedience, there's not much chance you'll die a death of obedience. A life of obedience would be reflected, as Paul pointed out, in humility, kindness, truth, and generosity. My questions became: *In any moment of any day, what in me needs to die so that Christ may be exalted? Am I willing to be that radically obedient to God?*

I realized I needed to go back to the beginning and find a working definition of obedience. I couldn't obey if I didn't know what God wanted me to do, so the first necessary component of obedience is to hear His voice. God uses all kinds of ways to communicate His presence and His will to people—a burning bush, pillars of clouds and fire, a whisper after an earthquake, a donkey, a finger writing on a wall, appearances of angels, and voices from heaven, to name only a few. But the way God has chosen to speak most clearly and most often is through the Scriptures. If we soak our minds and hearts in God's Word, we can be sure He will illumine His truth and reveal Himself to us there. Our task then becomes responding with the attitude of Jesus and obeying to the point of death—immediately, fully, and courageously.

WHAT IF?

As God led me to make a commitment to focus for a year on immediate obedience, I wondered, *What if God has something for me that's far bigger than I ever imagined?* I wasn't thinking of positions or power or possessions. I was considering the adventure of walking hand in hand with the sovereign, mighty, and gentle King of all. Could any adventure be more thrilling (and threatening) than this? What if God had specific assignments for me in the ordinary course of my day? What if I were sensitive enough to hear His whispers, and what if I were bold enough to act when I heard Him speak? Was it possible that I would experience the divine in the ordinary?

Through the course of the year—and every day since then—I have encountered God more fully than ever before. The commitment to listen and immediately obey has revolutionized how I view each day. My to-do list is no longer mundane; it's infused with the possibility that God may do something spectacular and unexpected if I sense His directive at any point. My meetings with people—scheduled or random—always carry the possibility that God may break into the ordinary and tell me to do something that changes a life.

These divine encounters may only last for a few seconds or a few minutes, so it's essential for me to respond instantly when I hear God's voice. Of course, I miss some of those "God moments," either because I'm confused about what I sense from God or because I'm too slow to respond. But I'm getting in a lot of practice! With each bold response, I become a little more receptive to hear Him, and I get a little more confident that it's worth it to have the attitude of Christ every moment of every day.

> God doesn't have to tell me what He's up to before I act, and I don't have to see definitive results after I obey.

God doesn't have to tell me what He's up to before I act, and I don't have to see definitive results after I obey. God just asks me to do as He instructs and leave the results to Him. That's what Jesus did. Everywhere He went, He did exactly what the Father told Him to do. But the results were, to say the least, mixed: some adored Him, some feared Him, and some despised Him. When I hear God's voice and obey to step into people's lives, I can expect some to be grateful, some to be confused, and some to think I've lost my mind. I'm okay with that.

FIRST STEPS

After my "year of immediate obedience" to understand and practice the principles on my own, I taught them to our church. The response has been more thrilling than I could have imagined. I couldn't be more excited about what God has been doing in and through our people as their spiritual ears are opened and they respond instantly to God's directives.

But I don't want you to make any commitments yet. Wait until you finish this book and then I will give you a 90-day challenge as an experiment. For three months, you will read the Scriptures, pray, and expect God to lead you. Like any new habit or skill, obedience has a learning curve. You'll get some things right, and you'll miss the mark sometimes. I'm still learning, and I expect to keep learning for the rest of my life.

Your journey, though, isn't designed to end after ninety days. I hope you'll make it a central priority of your life to listen and obey. There are no guarantees that God will speak at a certain time about a particular person or situation. We simply open our hearts to the fact that God longs to communicate His heart and intentions to us. If we listen and obey, a world of possibilities opens up before us.

People who practice immediate obedience are the ones we love to hang around. We listen to their stories and marvel at how God uses them. You can be one of those people. Give it a shot and see what happens. You have nothing to lose and everything to gain.

I have asked volunteers in our church to share their stories of immediate obedience. In every chapter, I will summarize how God has used them or let them tell their own stories. The first one is from a man named Phil.

Pastor Rod,

Last Friday my marketing director asked me to come to his office. He said he wanted me to take over a major account from someone who was retiring. It was a dream account. My commission would give me a big raise, and I would get to travel around the country. It was exactly the job I wanted!

The only problem was that the travel would take me away from home and prevent me from leading a ministry at the church. I told my boss I'd think about it over the weekend and get back to him.

At the time, I was one of the volunteer leaders of the high school ministry. Both of my sons were involved, and I loved doing something that had a direct impact on their spiritual development. I was really excited about seeing kids grow in their faith, but I would have to give up my time with them if I took the account. For that reason, I decided to turn it down.

When I told my boss, he told me that I was wasting a golden opportunity to advance my career. He told me, "You're going to close a lot of doors around here by not taking the job."

In the grand scheme of God's kingdom, my decision wasn't very big, but it was big to me. Before I told my boss about my choice, I spent most of Sunday night's sermon with knots in my stomach. I was on the verge of tears. It was the first time I had ever given up part of my future for the sake of ministry. It wasn't easy, and I didn't like it. I wondered if I was being a fool, but your message about immediate obedience rang in my ears. It was the right decision for a number of reasons.

It isn't a real sacrifice—like life or death—but for the first time I felt like I died to self in a big way.

Pastor Rod, that's my obedience story. Thank you so much for teaching us to respond to God.

Phil

1

IMMEDIATE OBEDIENCE . . .
ARE YOU KIDDING?

*"If we examine our consciences deliberately, clearly,
and in the presence of God, I think we're going to find out
that a whole lot of what we call 'struggling' is delayed obedience."*
—Elisabeth Elliott

E very believer can have a vibrant, dynamic, expectant connection with God and participate in fulfilling His purposes. My friend Randy probably has the least exciting job in the world. He leads a crew cleaning offices in the dead of night when no one is around. When Randy discovered the commitment to obey God and listen for His voice, it changed everything for him. He had seen his work as drudgery, but suddenly every night was filled with the possibility that God might whisper to him to have a divine encounter with someone who works for him.

I'm not suggesting that every moment of every day will be full of burning bush experiences. Even Moses only had one of those. But Moses became sensitive to the voice of God and committed to obey

Him, no matter how absurd His directions seemed—in confronting Pharaoh, leading the people through the Red Sea, climbing up a mountain quaking with fire, and countless other ways during forty years in the wilderness. At the burning bush, something in Moses changed. He became committed to God in a new and different way. He determined to obey God immediately no matter what the cost, and God did incredible things in him, for him, and through him.

A WHOLE NEW WORLD

In the same way, when we make a commitment to listen and obey, a world of possibilities opens in front of us. When I sit next to someone on an airplane or place my order in a coffee shop, I try to anticipate God's voice in each encounter. Sometimes I don't sense anything unusual, so I assume God simply wants me to represent Him with kindness and love. But I'm learning that sometimes God will give me special instructions. If I respond and do what He says, I get to participate in the supernatural event of God's using me to touch a person's heart. If I miss it for any reason, the moment passes and the opportunity is lost.

Being sensitive to God's voice and dedicated to respond immediately affects how I view every moment. Problems are no longer inconvenient hassles. Instead, they become open doors to connect with people I may not have met if the problem hadn't occurred. Routine activities are no longer boring because I realize God can turn any of them into something that changes a life. In a commitment to obey immediately, there are no mundane moments and no ordinary people. Every second is infused with incredible possibilities because God may show up and do something miraculous.

The most miraculous thing is that God is willing to use someone like me (and you) to be His hands, His voice, and His heart to share with the people we meet each day.

> Every second is infused with incredible possibilities because God may show up and do something miraculous.

The more I hear God's voice and see Him use me, the more I anticipate the next time He may give me directions. I don't want to miss a single time! I don't want any selfishness or impatience to distract from what God wants to do through me. For me, personal holiness isn't a demanding, oppressive commitment to rules. I simply don't want anything to interfere with the incredible connection I have with God! Holiness is much more about love than legalism (1 John 3:1–3).

When I was first learning the concept of immediate obedience, I was in a restaurant in Louisville, Kentucky, with three friends who are leaders in the Assemblies of God. Our waitress had tattoos on every exposed part of her body, and I would imagine she had a few others that were momentarily undercover. Her hair was dyed and spiked, and she had several piercings. Her physical appearance didn't bother me in the least. A number of people who look like her attend our church, and I want them to feel completely comfortable. The look on her face, however, sent a strong message that she was extremely unhappy. She looked angry . . . distracted . . . like she would rather be anywhere but waiting on us. After she took our order and walked away, I sensed the Lord tell me, "I want you to give her $100."

I inwardly reacted, "Oh, not now . . . not her!"

Then I sensed the Lord say, "That's not all. I want you to tell her why you're giving her the money."

Giving money wasn't a new concept to me. My father modeled generosity, and he taught me to carry cash to give away. He said that if you have to write a check or go to an ATM, you will talk yourself out of it. He recommended carrying cash so you can pull it out and give it without engaging in self-doubt. So at the restaurant that night, I had the money in my wallet. That wasn't the problem.

For me, the piercing question was this: How would it look to these three leaders for me to do something so out of the ordinary? I had known them for a while, but not that well. I didn't want them to think I was stupid or foolish or strange. Or worse, they might think I was trying to act super-spiritual. None of those options looked attractive, so I tried to talk God out of it.

I thought about offering to pay for dinner and adding $100 to the tip. I sensed God saying "No. That's not what I told you to do." I contemplated coming back to the restaurant after the four of us left to give her the money and talk to her then. Again, I knew God didn't want me to do that.

She came back to the table to bring our food. As the others ate and talked, I was totally preoccupied with my fears and doubts. I barely touched my dinner because I was so upset. I wasn't at all concerned about what she would think of me if I told her about the love of Christ, but I was terribly worried about the label these three men might put on me if they saw me give her some money and tell her about saving faith. I tried to reason my way out of it, but I was absolutely sure God had a purpose for putting this young woman on my heart.

The moment of truth came when she brought the check. I told the others, "I've got this." Then I turned to our waitress and said, "I've got something for you, but first I want to tell you a story."

She rolled her eyes and cocked her hips like she knew she had to listen but was already bored out of her mind. Then before I could say another word, she looked over at the next table and said, "I've got to take care of these people. I'll be back in a minute."

In the minute she was waiting on the other table, three sets of eyes bored through me. The other guys looked at me like they wondered if I had just escaped from an asylum, but I was finally convinced that I had to obey God and speak up. When she came back to our table, she resumed her defiant posture. I didn't try to be eloquent. I thought I might as well be honest and kind. I looked up at her and explained, "This year, I've sensed that every time God puts something on my heart, I need to obey Him. When we sat down, I felt God told me to give you something and tell you why I'm giving it to you." Now *four* sets of eyes were looking at me like I had lost my mind. I gave her the money and said simply, "God knows you, He loves you, and He's interested in you."

I didn't give her an extended gospel presentation. I felt God only wanted me to make a personal connection and tell her that He loves her. When she realized I had given her $100, her eyes lit up, and she almost shouted, "Oh, wow! This makes my day! It makes my week!

In fact, it makes my month!" After a brief pause, she announced, "I'm going to take this money to Vegas!"

I had done what God asked me to do, and I had to leave the response to Him. It would be a much better story if the spiked-hair waitress had fallen to her knees and said, "I've been waiting for someone to tell me about Jesus! I repent and turn my life over to Him!" But she didn't. As far as I know, the money I gave her was converted to quarters and shoved into slot machines. That's not my business. God only called me to listen and obey—and fight my fear that I would look stupid to the people watching me.

Amazingly, none of the three men with me said a word about my conversation and my gift to the waitress. I don't know if they were embarrassed, if they thought it was cool, or if they wondered if I was a nut case. Actually, lost people often feel more comfortable with spiritual sensitivity than believers. Many Christians think they have figured out how to make life work, and adventure with God isn't part of their equation.

COMMON FEARS

When I began this journey, I sometimes worried about "getting it wrong." I would wonder, *Was that thought from God, or was that just me?* I don't worry about that any more. I'm sure I get it wrong from time to time. Being wrong isn't a surprise when finite beings try to relate to the infinite God. All people have limitations. I certainly have mine. If I take action and later realize it was my idea instead of God's, it's still a good thing to be kind and generous to people. I'm far more concerned that I'll be spiritually insensitive and unable to hear God's voice. But even then, I'm certain that God delights to break through barriers and communicate with me, even when my hearing is becoming dulled (maybe *especially* when my spiritual ears are becoming dull).

My other concern is that I'll let my fear of what people think of me dictate my response to God. He is the Lord, not them. He is the King, not them. His agenda is far more important than theirs or mine. When people realize what I'm doing, many of them want to join me in learning to obey immediately after hearing God's voice. But others . . . not so much.

I was at a restaurant with a nationally known Christian leader when the Lord whispered to me to talk to the waiter about his life and show some kindness. As we talked, the leader sitting with me became visibly disturbed. As the seconds ticked by, his impatience grew exponentially. Finally, he interrupted my conversation with the waiter and blurted out, "I want some iced tea! Would you just get me some tea? I'm tired of waiting!" That man and I were running on two separate tracks. He was more concerned about getting his iced tea than showing God's love to the person God had brought into our lives at that moment. Before I criticize him for being selfish and insensitive, however, I need to ask myself how many times I've been more concerned about my petty wants than the people in front of me.

Hearing and responding to God's voice isn't a power trip. It doesn't give me license to be a jerk or be arrogant because "I've arrived" or "I'm

The better I am in tune with God, the more I am blown away by His tenderness, kindness, and compassion for people.

an insider with God." Just the opposite. The better I am in tune with God, the more I am blown away by His tenderness, kindness, and compassion for people. As I listen and obey, I get in touch with His incredible humility and grace.

IMMEDIACY AND AMAZEMENT

We live in a culture geared toward immediate gratification. Modern technology and conveniences promise we'll get exactly what we want, and we'll get it now! Immediacy, though, isn't just a modern phenomenon. In Mark's gospel he uses the terms "immediately," "at once," and "at that time" about forty times. His message was that Jesus was completely dedicated to the Father's mission, and He let nothing get in the way. Jesus had a sense of urgency. Even for the Creator of time, there was no time to lose: no reluctance, no excuses, and no delays.

Time wasn't the only thing Mark wanted to highlight. He identifies a common response of those who saw Jesus obey the Father instantly. They were often "amazed" (Mark 1:22, 27, 6:51, 10:24). In the same way, when you practice immediate obedience, at least two people will be amazed—you, and the person to whom you show the love and power of Christ.

Immediate obedience almost always provokes genuine amazement at the glory, kindness, and presence of God. People aren't used to seeing Christians really living out their faith. Their concept of Christianity is a bunch of people who are *against* all kinds of things and *for* almost nothing. Sadly, we have given them plenty of reasons to have this perception of us! British philosopher and theologian G. K. Chesterton famously quipped, "Christianity has not been tried and found wanting; it has been found difficult and left untried."[3]

Christianity is difficult precisely because it asks us to have the attitude of Christ, to live in humility, and to die to our selfish desires all day every day. Those are not easy things to do. But when someone has the courage to live that way, the world sits up and notices. It's truly amazing!

Obedience to God always involves other people. God asks us to take a minute to show kindness to someone who has been overlooked, to give money to a person in trouble, or to surprise someone with an act of radical love. Even when God tells us to stop some behavior that is self-destructive, our response becomes a public display of obedience because people notice. Obedience always amazes those who observe us.

WAIT A MINUTE!

Does the idea of listening for the voice of God with a commitment to obey Him immediately make you more than a little nervous? Join the club! I understand. I've been there. In fact, I spent a year immersed in this concept before I was willing to talk about it to anyone but Cindy and my closest friends. The inherent questions that are part of the package include:

- What in the world will God ask me to do?
- How can I be certain it's His voice I hear?

- What will it cost me?
- What changes will I have to make to be able to listen more intently?
- Is this really possible? (After all, I don't hear a lot of others talking this way.)
- Am I going to look like a certified nut?

In my own experience, and now in the lives of those who are learning to apply this principle, I've noticed that our fears are often misplaced. We're afraid of what we might lose if we obey God, but we should be more concerned about what we'll lose if we *don't* obey! For some strange reason, many people assume that their dedication to obey God gives Him permission to make their lives miserable. But that's Satan's goal, not God's. Jesus explained how Satan's motives contrast with His: "The thief comes only to steal and kill and destroy; I have come that they may have life, and have it to the full. I am the good shepherd. The good shepherd lays down his life for the sheep" (John 10:10–11).

How do parents respond when their children say, "Mom and Dad, I love you and I trust you so much that I'll do anything you want me to do"? After they pick themselves off the floor, the parents shower their kids with love. God is the perfect parent. He's infinitely wise, and His plans are far bigger and more complicated than we can ever fathom, so sometimes we simply won't understand what He's up to. But when we begin to grasp the depth of His love and the extent of His power, we will realize our commitment to obey Him positions us right in the middle of His will, His love, and His blessings.

EYES TO SEE

Most of us like guarantees, but two risks of obeying God's voice are not having answers and not being able to predict outcomes. Most of the time, when God whispers to give me directions I have no clue what's going on in the person's life, and I certainly don't know what his or her response will be. Sometimes the person's heart melts on the spot, and I realize this was the perfectly prepared divine moment to meet that person's need. But more often, the recipient thinks I'm odd or takes the money to Vegas! There are no guarantees with immediate obedience, but there are plenty of thrills.

As people in our church have practiced listening and responding to God, they've seen encouraging results. I love to hear their stories—and sometimes I hear "the other side of the story" from the recipients affected by their sensitivity to God. Every Sunday I go to our welcome center to greet people who are attending our church for the first time. I often ask how they heard about our church. One week I met a lady who had a puzzled expression on her face. I introduced myself, and she told me, "I was at the gas station yesterday. A man came up to me and said God had told him to buy my gas. I was stunned. No one had ever done anything like that for me before. I asked him where he went to church—I wanted to know what kind of church produces people who are so generous . . . and so strange. He told me about your church. I wanted to come this morning to see what had happened in his life." I smiled and told her I was glad to have her join us.

As God gives us eyes to see—really *see*—the people around us, He often directs us to give one of two things (or both): kindness and money. The most common emotion attributed to Jesus in the Gospels is compassion. Again and again, the writers tell us Jesus was moved with compassion for those who were hurting and hopeless. It's only logical that when His Spirit moves us, we will express Jesus' compassion and kindness to people in need as we encounter them.

Similarly, the topic of money was important to Jesus. He talked about it more than almost any other subject—not because He was obsessed with the possessions, positions, and the power money can bring, but because *we* are! In His most famous sermon, Jesus told the crowd, "Do not store up for yourselves treasures on earth, where moths and vermin destroy, and where thieves break in and steal. But store up for yourselves treasures in heaven, where moths and vermin do not destroy, and where thieves do not break in and steal. For where your treasure is, there your heart will be also" (Matt. 6:19–21).

As you look at advertising and listen to friends, you quickly realize that money plays a central role in the hearts and minds of most people on the planet. When we give away what most people pursue and hoard, they're shocked, and they want to know what makes us tick. They realize we're serving a different Master. Generosity is the perfect platform to talk about God's most generous gift: His Son's sacrificial payment for unworthy sinners.

Quite often, compassion and generosity go hand in hand. When the weather forecast predicted an ice storm headed for Little Rock, Kenny Brock took three gas cans to be filled up so he could run his generator if the power failed. As he was pumping the gas, he noticed a woman who seemed to be in distress. She was filling up her car, but she was weeping.

Kenny went over and asked if he could help. She asked for directions to the hospital. Kenny told her how to get there and then said, "If you'll wait a couple of minutes, I'll let you follow me." But before he knew it, she took off down the road. At that moment, Kenny sensed God telling him something totally implausible: "She needs help. Take your gas cans home and go find her."

Kenny finished pumping the gas and took the cans home. When he arrived and opened the garage, his daughter and his wife were having an argument and wanted him to resolve it. He told them, "I'll have to come back to that later. Right now, I'm on a mission! No time to explain." He got back in his truck and sped down the highway. He knew the direction the distraught woman had gone, but he had no idea if she had made it to the hospital—especially in her emotional state.

He didn't see her on the five-mile trip to the hospital, but he soon found her near her car in the parking lot. He could tell she was confused. Kenny took her to the emergency room and waited with her until the nurse called her back. As they waited, she told him she wanted to tell a friend in California that she was sick. Kenny got her friend's number and called to inform her.

Kenny sat in the waiting room until the lady came out. She still looked very confused, so he made sure she had a place to stay. He gave her some money for food, and wrote down his number in case she needed any more help. Kenny had quite an adventure that night. It happened because he was sensitive to God's voice and moved with compassion to care for a stranger.

DECIDE IN ADVANCE

Early in my year of immediate obedience, I realized I couldn't wait to decide if I would obey after I heard God speak to me. If I made a habit of waiting, I would waste a lot of time trying to determine if I had heard correctly and if I even wanted to respond, so I would miss many opportunities. Jesus' attitude was a predetermined commitment to obey the Father's will no matter what He said to do or where He said to go. I had to make a predetermined commitment, too. No matter what God told me, my answer was going to be "Yes!" I took "No," "Wait a minute," and "Let me think about it" off the table.

> Jesus' attitude was a predetermined commitment to obey the Father's will no matter what He said to do or where He said to go.

Before we hear God's voice, we decide that everything we are and everything we have is entirely His. This is "open-handed living." We don't own any of it; we're just taking care of it so it'll be ready when God says He wants to use it. Our schedule is God's, our money is God's, our possessions are God's, our talents are God's, our free time is God's, and our reputation is God's. If we don't make this decision in advance, we'll resent it when God tells us to give generously, and we'll argue with Him when He instructs us to go out of our way to help someone.

Thankfully, Jesus didn't resent going to the cross to pay the ultimate price for us. He stepped out of the glory and beauty of heaven with the clear knowledge that He wouldn't just be *inconvenienced* for helping us, but He would be *tortured and killed* for our sake. He often predicted His death, but He "set His face like flint" to suffer and die for us (Isa. 50:7, Luke 9:51).

This may seem like a grim mindset, but it's not. Jesus was the happiest person who ever lived. He delighted in seeing lepers healed, the lame walk, the dead raised, and all kinds of people experience His forgiveness. As He followed the Father's path, He endured betrayal, plots, and misunderstanding, but His obedience to the Father wasn't based on the responses of people. It was determined before the incarnation. No matter the individual reaction of people to Him and His message, He focused on the Father and trusted and obeyed.

The writer to the Hebrews reminds us, "Let us run with perseverance the race marked out for us, fixing our eyes on Jesus, the pioneer and perfecter of faith. For the joy set before him he endured the cross, scorning its shame, and sat down at the right hand of the throne of God" (Heb. 12:1–2). "The joy set before him" was us! To Jesus, you are worth more than the stars in the skies and all the gold and diamonds in the world. Jesus delighted in doing the Father's will and showering His love on people. In the same way, when your heart is aligned with His, you'll delight in doing His will—fully and immediately—and seeing Him use you to touch the lives of those around you.

NO LIMITATIONS, NO EXCEPTIONS

Some Christians conclude that the invitation and challenge to immediate obedience must be only for pastors, missionaries, desert fathers, monks, and super-spiritual saints. They're wrong. God wants every one of His children to enjoy this kind of closeness, this kind of excitement, and this kind of wonder in seeing Him work in and through them. The joy of immediate obedience is available for those who have been wandering through each day, wondering if their lives matter at all. They're tired of living an empty, confusing, meaningless existence. At some point, they wonder, "God, do You really have a purpose for me? Is there something more than what I've been experiencing?"

A life of intimacy, joy, and power through immediate obedience to God has no boundaries regarding race, culture, age, gender, personality, career, or socioeconomics. God's invitation is open to everyone. Quite often, God uses the obedience of a few to break down the barriers of an entire culture. Whites reach out to African-Americans, Hispanics are generous to whites, cautious people have a word of love for entrepreneurs, and poor people step in to comfort rich people in distress. God is incredibly creative. I think He smiles as He leads people to do things they would never have dreamed of doing on their own. All it takes is a willing heart, a listening ear, and a predetermined choice to obey whatever God whispers to us.

God is waiting for ordinary people to sign up for the adventure of a lifetime: to know Him more intimately, hear Him more clearly, and step out to do whatever He directs. Immediate obedience is for:

- The teacher who has been annoyed by a problem student, but realizes God may have put that child in her classroom for a purpose.

- The businessman whose flight is delayed, who prays, "Lord, forgive me for griping about the inconvenience of the plane being late. Do You have something for me here and now?" He realizes the delay just may be part of God's plan for him to have a meaningful conversation with the guy in the next seat.

- The high school student who gets up in the morning and prays, "Lord, speak to me today. I'm listening, and I'll obey You." When she walks into the cafeteria at lunch, she notices a girl sitting alone—and suddenly realizes she has been sitting alone every day for the past month or so. She hears God say, "Go over and sit with her. She needs a friend."

- The stressed-out single mom who feels overwhelmed by all the pressures of work and caring for her kids but begins to see every day at work and at home infused with opportunities for "God moments." Her life and her goals suddenly become meaningful.

- Ordinary people who have trouble keeping up with their bills, but discover the joy and wonder of responding to God's directives to give generously to those in need. At first they're afraid God will let them down and they will go broke, but they soon realize that being sensitive to God and generous with people puts them in touch with God's unlimited resources of blessing.

- Poor people and rich people, slow and smart, plain and beautiful, the down-and-out and the up-and-coming, every person who has failed miserably and wants another chance, and everyone who thirsts for God.

The Bible is a series of accounts of ordinary people who heard God's voice and responded in faith to whatever He told them to do. They weren't Supermen and Wonder Women. They were normal people with the same hopes and fears we have, but they answered when they heard God speak—and amazing things happened.

In fact, there are no amazing stories in the Bible that don't include immediate obedience. Of course, there are plenty of examples of sin, failure, rebellion, betrayal, selfishness, and foolishness. Some people closed their ears to God and refused to respond in faith to His voice. But don't be misled: the heroes of the Bible were just like you and me. Abraham lied about Sarah being his wife when he got in a tight spot. Moses murdered an Egyptian and then had to go on the lam. Peter swore allegiance to Jesus but denied Him three times before morning. Yet God used these imperfect people to accomplish great things. Other countless men and women through the ages have put their mistakes and weaknesses behind them, eventually emulating the attitude of Jesus by becoming obedient to the point of death. They swapped their selfish agendas to grab God's agenda of intimacy and immediacy.

> There are no amazing stories in the Bible that don't include immediate obedience.

Do you want an amazing life? Make a commitment to immediate obedience. Your life will never be the same. I guarantee it.

Sue discovered that God's whispers are sometimes confusing, but always right on target to touch a heart and meet a need.

Pastor Rod,

A few years ago I had a close friend who was pregnant. As Christmas approached and I was praying, I felt God impress on my heart that I should bless my friend with money to spend on maternity clothes. Instantly, I assumed the idea couldn't be from God. It seemed weird for God to ask me to give money for a friend's clothes. In my mind, if God was going to impress my heart to give money, it should be something big and spiritual, like missions, a church plant, or to care for a starving family. So as quickly as God put the thought on my heart, I let it leave me.

Only the thought didn't leave. I saw my friend many times during the next three weeks—far more often than our paths usually cross. Each time I remembered God's whispered message, but each time I chose to ignore Him. Still, I had this nagging feeling . . .

After three weeks I couldn't take it anymore. One Sunday morning I went up to her and handed her some cash. I blurted out, "God told me to give this to you. And as weird as it is, I think He wants you to spend it on you. He wants you to use it for maternity clothes, and He wants you to know He is taking care of your every need!"

Big tears welled up in her eyes. I only gave her about ten seconds before I followed with a big apology. I told her the backstory about how God had spoken to me weeks ago, but I hadn't listened to His voice. She was my friend, so I wanted to be honest. I admitted my disobedience and told her I was sorry I had missed the opportunity for God to use me to reach out to her.

For both of us, it was an amazing moment. That day we both learned to trust God in different ways. I don't think it had anything to do with money for either of us. It was about God speaking and me listening. It's a day I'll never forget.

Sue

———

At the end of each chapter, you'll find some questions to stimulate personal reflection and group discussion. Don't rush through these. The goal isn't to fill in the blanks quickly. It's to think deeply and invite God to work in your heart.

CONSIDER THIS . . .

1. How would you define and describe "immediate obedience"?

2. Read Philippians 2:1–11. What is the attitude Paul describes in the first four verses? How does Jesus exemplify this attitude in verses 5 through 8?

3. Does the idea of being sensitive to God's voice and instantly responding make you a little nervous (or maybe more than a little nervous!)? What are your fears? How do the Introduction and Chapter 1 address them?

4. Why is it essential to decide in advance to obey when you hear God's whisper or sense His nudge?

5. Are you a candidate for this lifestyle? Why or why not? If so, what has led you to want this much of God? If not, what disqualifies you?

6. What do you hope God does in your life through this book?

2

GOD SPEAKS

"Two facts about the Triune Jehovah are assumed, if not actually stated, in every single biblical passage. The first is that He is king—absolute monarch of the universe, ordering all its affairs, working out His will in all that happens within it. The second fact is that He speaks—uttering words that express His will in order to cause it to be done."

—J. I. Packer

God may whisper to us to prompt us to show kindness to family members, call a friend across the country, or give a generous gift to someone we meet in passing. Sometimes He asks us to open our eyes to notice people we walk past every day.

As our family became more sensitive to the Spirit's voice, Cindy felt the Lord tell her that He wanted us to really notice the hidden people in our lives. Every Christmas season we ask our boys to tell us how much of the money we've allotted for their Christmas presents they want to give away. The amounts vary from year to year, but they're always generous. Cindy realized this would be the perfect opportunity to combine our habit of *giving* with a greater sense of *noticing*. As a family Christmas project, we put money in envelopes and asked God to direct us to the people to receive the gifts. And as He had previously instructed me

As our family is learning to listen and obey, we have found the experience wonderfully liberating and incredibly adventurous.

about the waitress, He also directed us to tell the recipients why we were giving them the gifts—in this case, by writing notes to them.

We asked God to put particular people on our hearts, and He did. The week before Christmas we staked out our trashcans so we would be ready when the truck came by. When the sanitation workers picked up our trash, we jumped out to give them envelopes with $100 bills and personal messages. We told them how much we appreciated their service and sent them on their way. They were as shocked as we were thrilled! It was magnificent! (These days if you drive down our street after the truck has come by, you will see trash cans on their side, in the gutter, and in yards—except at our house. The workers get off the truck, take our cans to our garage, and neatly line them up as their way of saying "Thank you!" I'm sure our neighbors wonder what's going on!)

Cindy and I also gave money and notes to the lady who works at the dry cleaners, the pharmacy tech where we get our prescriptions filled, and the teller at the bank. They are people we often see, but who had previously just been cogs in the machinery of our lives. After God put the idea on Cindy's heart, they became people with hopes and hurts, dreams and dreads—people God loves . . . and suddenly, people *we* really loved. The response to our Christmas giving was amazing. We received hugs, tears, beautiful notes, and cards. It made Christmas really special.

As our family is learning to listen and obey, we have found the experience wonderfully liberating and incredibly adventurous. It's liberating because we're no longer shackled to dull habits that had seemed meaningful in the past but had lost their flavor. And it's adventurous because we never know when God might speak and lead us to do something daring. Adventures always involve risk. Immediate obedience includes many risks: primarily being wrong and looking foolish. We're learning that the benefits far outweigh those risks.

THE KING SPEAKS

We live in an individualistic culture in a representative democracy. We Americans pride ourselves on our independence. When we don't like what our politicians are doing, we rise up and vote them out of office. Our system of government is established "of the people, by the people, and for the people." One of the most important (and often surprising) truths about our faith is that God's kingdom is different . . . very different.

The Bible tells us that God is the sovereign ruler, not just of a community or a nation, but of the vast expanse of the universe. Many passages describe God's power and authority, but one of my favorites is Isaiah 40. Isaiah explained that God is as tender as a shepherd caring for newborn lambs, but His might and wisdom are beyond comprehension. We marvel at the size of the oceans, but God "has measured the waters in the hollow of his hand." And we have trouble conceiving a universe measured in light-years, each of which is almost six trillion miles, but God "marked off the heavens" by the width of His hand

(Isa. 40:12). We may think our scientists and philosophers are smart, but God is omniscient—He knows absolutely everything . . . in your heart and mine, and in the atoms in the farthest galaxies (vv. 13–14). Nations, empires, and political structures come and go in decades or centuries, but they are all just "a drop in a bucket" and "dust on the scales" of God's sweeping plans (vv. 15–17). Isaiah asks, "With whom, then, will you compare God?" (v. 18) He makes a list of the most powerful things on earth, and he concludes that compared to the glory, power, and authority of Almighty God, all those things are no more than the leftovers of threshed grain, worthless and blowing in the winds of time (vv. 19–24).

Centuries later, Handel began his epic *Messiah* with passages from Isaiah 40, and in a stirring crescendo he built toward the famous chorus that proclaims,

> "For the Lord God omnipotent reigneth.
> Hallelujah! Hallelujah! Hallelujah! Hallelujah!
> For the Lord God omnipotent reigneth.
> Hallelujah! Hallelujah! Hallelujah! Hallelujah!
> The kingdom of this world
> Is become the kingdom of our Lord,
> And of His Christ, and of His Christ;
> And He shall reign for ever and ever."[4]

Some people assume that because they don't understand what God is up to, they shouldn't trust Him. They think understanding is a prerequisite of faith. But if we could understand everything the God of infinite power and wisdom was doing, either we would have to be infinite too, or He would have to be as limited as we are. It's only logical that there will be times (plenty of times) when God is preparing something so vast, so wonderful, and so mysterious that our minds are simply too small to comprehend His plans. Some people then conclude that God demands that we have "blind faith." No, He wants us to have wide-eyed wonder! He invites us to be amazed at His mighty power, piercing wisdom, and mysterious plans. With faith inspired by His greatness and goodness, we put our lives in His hands even when we don't have a clue what He's up to.

If we capture even a glimmer of God's majesty, we will want His magnificent, wise plans instead of insisting on our own. We won't resent it when God's plans don't match up with ours. Instead, we will realize we were settling for something far less worthy, exciting, and effective than His plans to prosper us and use us to reclaim people for His sake.

Our King, though, doesn't sit in a faraway corner of the universe hoping we don't make too much of a mess of our lives. He is involved with us all day every day. As we have seen, our joy and task is to live in a way that brings God's kingdom "to earth as it is in heaven." Heaven isn't "out there" somewhere; it's a different dimension of God's glory and presence around us now. Before Jesus ascended back to the Father, He told His disciples, "All authority in heaven and on earth has been given to me. Therefore go and make disciples of all nations, baptizing them in the name of the Father and of the Son and of the Holy Spirit, and teaching them to obey everything I have commanded you. And surely I am with you always, to the very end of the age" (Matt. 28:18–20). He is with us, too.

Theologians explain that God is *transcendent* (far above anything we can imagine) and *imminent* (as close as our breath). He is the atmosphere of our existence at every moment of every day, at our best and at our worst. The more we realize we live *in* Him, the more we want to live *for* Him.

And the infinitely wise and powerful God, the King of glory, communicates with His people. It's amazing but true. Imagine how you would feel if your caller ID showed the President was calling you—or Bono or Justin Timberlake or Beyoncé or Labron James or someone else you admire. You would be amazed that person wanted to talk to you. You would be thrilled and hang on the person's every word.

You're probably not going to get a call from any of those people, but I can guarantee you this: the God of glory is definitely calling you. Someone far wiser, stronger, and more loving than anyone you can imagine wants to connect with you. Pick up the phone!

God has gone to great lengths to prove Himself to us. A passage in Philippians tells us that Jesus "emptied himself" and paid the ultimate price for us. The lyrics of a great hymn put it this way:

> "He left His Father's throne above
> So free, so infinite His grace—
> Emptied Himself of all but love,
> And bled for Adam's helpless race:
> 'Tis mercy all, immense and free,
> For O my God, it found out me!"[5]

Since God went to such lengths and paid such a high price to show His love to us, doesn't it make sense that He longs to make sure we experience His wonderful presence, love, and power? Jesus invites us, "Ask and it will be given to you; seek and you will find; knock and the door will be opened to you. For everyone who asks receives; the one who seeks finds; and to the one who knocks, the door will be opened" (Matt. 7:7-8).

One of the metaphors Jesus used to describe His relationship with believers is of a shepherd caring for his sheep. This, of course, is a reflection of Isaiah's description centuries earlier about God being a tender, attentive, powerful shepherd. In the first century, virtually everyone knew the intricacies of how to tend sheep. They didn't use brands to identify each flock like cattlemen do today. Hot irons aren't good for the wool. Instead, the sheep followed the voice of their shepherd. Even if several flocks mingled together, a shepherd could call and his sheep would follow him.

In a famous passage in John's gospel, Jesus claims to be the Jehovah of Isaiah: "I am the good shepherd; I know my sheep and my sheep know me" (John 10:14). He then explains His intimate connection with those in His flock: "My sheep listen to my voice; I know them, and they follow me" (John 10: 27).

Our King is more powerful than we can imagine, and He longs to be intimately involved in leading us. We are invited to come near to "God's throne of grace" (Heb. 4:16). If we will listen, we will hear Him. And when we hear Him, we need to follow.

"I KNOW BETTER"

To learn to listen and obey, we have to be honest about our culture's negative impact on our expectations of God. Many people see Him as more of a Santa Claus than a sovereign King, more of a waiter to meet all our desires than one who inspires wonder, more a negotiator with whom we can make deals than the Lord we worship. If we see Him as less than the mighty, loving, sovereign King of the universe, we will assume our plans are better than His plans, our desires are more important than His purposes, and our comfort is more essential than His kingdom. In other words, if we think we know better than God how our lives ought to go, we won't listen very well, and we certainly won't obey Him if it seems the least bit inconvenient.

People think they know better than God about their relationships, their finances, their goals and purposes, their lifestyles, and every other aspect of life. Their wrong assumptions show up in many ways, but chiefly through their misplaced priorities and their level of worry. They invest a lot of time and money in things that don't matter to God's kingdom, and they can't seem to find time to study God's Word, pray more than brief "rocket prayers," encourage others and be encouraged, or care for those in need. They don't give more than the minimum their consciences can bear.

And they worry. It's good and right to be genuinely concerned about problems and needs, but worry is categorically different. At its heart, worry is based on the conclusion that we know better than God how our lives should go—and that He's getting it wrong! In fact, all sin is the result of assuming that we can manage our destinies better than

God can direct them. We ignore the King who died to show His love for us, and instead, we listen to the voices of our culture that promise fulfillment, joy, and love. No matter how many lives they see that are train wrecks, many people think, "Maybe so, but I can make it work!"

The key to a thrilling life of being sensitive to the voice of God and immediately obeying Him is the firm belief that God's plan for our lives is fundamentally better than anything we can dream up.

> The key to a thrilling life of being sensitive to the voice of God and immediately obeying Him is the firm belief that God's plan for our lives is fundamentally better than anything we can dream up.

What if the God of creation actually wants a real, dynamic relationship with you? Are you ready?

What if God wants to give you directions—personally, individually, and specifically? Is that even possible?

Do you want to hear His voice and know His plans, or do you think your plans are better?

If He tells you to do something you don't understand, can you imagine that the God who spun the universe into existence and has all knowledge might know more than you? Can you trust Him even when you don't comprehend His purpose?

From beginning to end, the Bible is a story of a King who speaks. He's already present in every place and every moment of your life. That's an awesome fact, one that scares us to death! But He doesn't demand that you have everything right in your life before He speaks to you. He's incredibly kind and patient. He knows you're flawed—we're all as dumb as sheep! But He still whispers and shouts, and He wants a two-way conversation with you.

God has a divine plan for all of us—not just pastors and missionaries, but maids, clerks, laborers, students, businesspeople, bankers, and stay-at-home moms. If we listen, God will lead us in unfolding clarity about how He wants to use us as His partners in the greatest enterprise the world has ever known: bringing His kingdom into the hearts of countless people in our homes and communities . . . and around the world.

AVOID THE POWER PLAY

Even at this early point in the book, I suspect some people already have their hands up in caution, backing away from the idea of God speaking to people. They're resistant for a good reason: they have seen this language misused too many times. Various pastors, leaders, parents, and friends have told them, "God told me that you're supposed to do this or that." The statement is often made in a way that doesn't allow for any rebuttal . . . or even a question. If God said it, it's final!

I'm with the cautious readers. I've heard people say some of the wackiest things with the preface, "God told me" or "The Lord spoke to me." These people have told me who to hire and who to fire, what to say in my preaching, how to parent my kids, the direction our church should go, and how we should use our money. The list is almost endless.

Because "God told me" has been used to control and manipu-
late people, it's wise to be wary. The "God card" is the ultimate trump
card—whoever plays it wins. The implication is that if we don't jump
to do what the person claims God says, we're being disobedient to
God—so a guilt trip is added to the spiritual manipulation. This kind of
language denies others the right to disagree. After all, who has the guts
to disagree with God?

Sadly, I've watched people wield this oppressive power over others,
and I've seen the damage it can inflict. Those who were manipulated
often did what they were told, but out of fear, not love and confidence
in God's gracious plan.

No matter how definitely and/or defiantly others insist that God
has spoken to them about our church or me, I never take what they say
at face value. I evaluate the source. If a friend I trust tells me God has
said something, I listen very carefully. But if the person seems to be on
a power trip to prove his spirituality and have some kind of control over
me, I discount the messenger. I may still ask God if the message has
any validity, but I'm understandably hesitant to blindly accept what that
person has said (or demanded) in God's name.

However, the other side of this equation is that many people refuse
to say, "God told me" because they're afraid of being wrong. They don't
want to make a dramatic statement and then see their efforts fail. This
would open them to ridicule, and they can't stand that!

Hearing from God isn't an exact science. It's a relationship with
someone far beyond the realm of our comprehension who longs to

communicate with us. For that reason, we're going to get it wrong sometimes. When that happens, we need to be humble, not defensive or depressed. We can learn from our mistakes and then ask God to make us better listeners.

If we pay attention to our culture, we realize people have a built-in desire to connect with the supernatural.

- They call psychic hotlines.
- They think the message in their fortune cookie is real and personal.
- They make decisions based on their horoscopes.
- They download apps that predict when and how they will die.
- They go to palm readers and use Ouija boards.
- They Google "how to know the future" and find over three million sites.
- They think they see Jesus' image on a piece of French toast.

There's a better way to connect. We humbly open our hearts to the King who has proven His love and expect Him to share His heart with us. We can expect crazy, power-hungry people to abuse the concept, but we don't need to let them ruin our sensitivity to hearing God's voice.

HOW DOES GOD SPEAK?

The pages of Scripture show us that God isn't limited in how He communicates with people. From walking with Adam and Eve in the garden, to the rainbow, to tablets of stone, to prophets passing along God's messages of glory and doom, God has used all kinds of communication methods.

After I invited my church family to join me in the adventure of immediate obedience and asked them to send notes to describe their experiences, many of their responses began something like this: "Pastor Rod, I've never heard God speak in an audible voice, but this is how He spoke to me." I realized that an audible voice must be "the gold standard" of how people hope God will speak to them. But the gold standard isn't a voice from heaven; it's the Bible sitting on our bedside tables.

Let's look at the most common ways God communicates with people, beginning with the Scriptures.

The Bible: The Gold Standard

The Scriptures are "the Word of God," the way He speaks to all of us all the time. Christians often assume it's more spiritual (and more impressive) to be able to claim a spectacular, dramatic, and unusual source for God's voice, but the fact that God has spoken—and continues to speak—through the pages of Scripture is spectacular enough for me!

> The Bible is our first priority and the most common source of hearing God's instructions.

The Bible is our first priority and the most common source of hearing God's instructions. I don't know anyone who is genuinely sensitive to the Spirit's voice who hasn't developed the habit of feasting on God's

Word. As I help others learn to practice immediate obedience, I see a pattern. If they don't study the Scriptures and respond in faith to God's truth, they can't expect Him to use the more uncommon means of impressions, signs, dreams, and desires.

Some people dust off their twelve-pound, gold-edged monster of a Bible and complain, "It's huge, it's complicated, and I can't understand what it's saying!" Yes, it's big. No question about that. Complicated? Sure, it addresses the full scope of human dreams and follies, and it covers the sweep of creation, the fall into sin, redemption, and restoration in the new heavens and new earth. It was written thousands of years ago in cultures that predated the industrial and technological revolutions. But the Bible's insights into the human condition are as fresh and accurate as the most perceptive psychologists today.

Of course, if you have an older translation, don't be surprised if you find it tough sledding. Locate a newer version: the *New International Version* (NIV), *The Message,* or the *English Standard Version* (ESV). They are easy to read, and if you get a study Bible you will also have access to helpful notes. Like learning any new language or skill, there's a learning curve, so be patient. Start with the Gospel of John and ask God to reveal Himself to you. He will. You can count on it.

Many people bring preconceptions when they begin to read the Bible. They read a page or two and announce, "God wants me to be happy!" Really? I don't see that promised anywhere in the Book. God wants us to know, love, and follow Him, and He promises to make our lives full and meaningful. He never promises to protect us from suffering, but He promises to use everything that touches our lives to deepen our faith, shape our character, and draw us closer to Him.

The Bible doesn't tell you which car to drive or which movie to see, but it reminds you to be a wise steward of the resources God puts in your hands and to fill your mind and heart with "whatever is true, whatever is noble, whatever is right, whatever is pure, whatever is lovely, whatever is admirable" (Phil. 4:8). Many directives are crystal clear, such as the instructions Paul includes in his letter to the Ephesians (4:25–32): don't lie, but speak the truth; don't sin in your anger, but express it appropriately and make sure it doesn't take root; don't steal, but work and give generously; don't use words as weapons, but use them to build people up; don't let bitterness ruin you and your relationships, but be kind and forgiving, just like Jesus. If you follow the unmistakable directives in the Bible, you can be sure God will lead you as we tackle the gray areas of life.

The Bible isn't just a book. It has divine power to open our hearts to truth (called "illumination"). It will teach us, identify sins and immaturity, correct us, and change us from the inside out (2 Tim. 3:16–17). As we read the Scriptures, God uses them to expose our deepest secrets— not to punish us, but to give us an opportunity to repent. The writer to the Hebrews tells us, "For the word of God is alive and active. Sharper than any double-edged sword, it penetrates even to dividing soul and spirit, joints and marrow; it judges the thoughts and attitudes of the heart. Nothing in all creation is hidden from God's sight. Everything is uncovered and laid bare before the eyes of him to whom we must give account" (Heb. 4:12–13). When God "uncovers" the hidden motives and desires of our hearts, He is inviting us to experience even more of His grace and power.

Again and again throughout the Bible, God reminds us of His patient, compassionate, forgiving love for us. He could have blasted us off the face of the earth for our betrayal and indifference, but instead He invites us to come back to Him and experience His grace—no matter who we are and no matter what we've done.

A lot of people get caught up looking for spectacular spiritual experiences. They want a special word from God just to them. I've got good news: God has given each of us a book full of special words! Devour them, soak them into your heart, and marvel at God's ability to impart His truth directly to you each day.

Impressions

God often speaks to me through impressions. As I read, study, worship, pray, and talk to friends about the Lord, a thought sometimes breaks into my consciousness, or I have a certainly feeling about a person or an event. In those times, I sense that God wants me to do or say something, and I need to obey.

I believe the Holy Spirit is the one who prompts those impressions. Several passages in the New Testament tell us we have been adopted by God. Children who love their parents often know what the parents are thinking before a word is said. That's the way impressions sometimes work. As we develop an intimate relationship with our Heavenly Father, we sense what He's up to and what He wants us to do.

Of course, some people are more intuitive than others, but all of us can develop the kind of relationship with God that is sensitive to His nudges.

> As we develop an intimate relationship with our Heavenly Father, we sense what He's up to and what He wants us to do.

Peace

One of the ways God shows us His will is by the presence or absence of peace. We need to be careful, though, because this isn't a perfect indicator. When God gives me an impression to do something, I may be scared to death! However, even in my fear, there's a sense of rightness about it. That's the kind of peace Jesus promised (John 14:27).

Paul told the Colossians, "Let the peace of Christ rule in your hearts" (Col. 3:15). The word "rule" used here is like an umpire calling balls and strikes. God's peace gives us signals about what's right and what's wrong. There are times when Cindy and I make plans, but one or both of us come back and say, "Wait a minute. I don't feel right about this. I'm not sure what it is, but there's something in my spirit that's unsettled." We stop, pray, and reevaluate our decision.

If you make a plan and start to implement it, but you don't have a sense that is what God wants you to do, stop right there. Try to determine whether your feeling is fear of the unknown or the absence of God's stamp of approval. The two may look and feel the same, but they're different. It will take some discernment to tell them apart.

Desires

As we walk with God and His heart increasingly captures ours, we will want more of what He wants and value what He values. We will learn to live in alignment with the Spirit. When we begin our journey with God, it's understandable to have conflicting desires. We've loved the things of the world for a long time—prestige, possessions, power, and comfort—but we begin to realize those things only have value if they're in second (or third) place on our priority list. Jesus acknowledged the need for clothing, shelter, and food, but He said, "Seek first [God's] kingdom and his righteousness, and all these things will be given to you as well" (Matt. 6:33).

King David wrote, "Take delight in the LORD, and he will give you the desires of your heart" (Ps. 37:4). He wasn't talking about a cruise or a Ferrari! When our chief delight is the love of God and the wonder of His grace toward us, the desires of our hearts radically shift. Our hearts begin to break when we encounter suffering, poverty, abuse, and death . . . and they sing when we see God transform lives, restore families, and bring resources to those in need.

If we aren't delighting in the Lord, we need to be skeptical about our desires because they'll almost always be self-centered. But the more thrilled we are to be God's beloved children, the more we see our hopes and dreams changing, and the more we become like Him.

Godly Wisdom

The Lord often inspires and challenges us through the counsel of authorities and friends. This kind of input includes a wide spectrum from casual conversation to someone giving us a word from the Lord.

Quite often I receive feedback and advice from Cindy, our church staff, and friends here and across the country. I treasure their support and honesty. I also value the input from people in authority over me. I realize God has put them in my life to give me direction, so I listen very carefully to what they say. But as I have said, when other people step into my life with what they say is an authoritative word from God, I always evaluate the source.

If someone tells you, "God told me," you don't have to immediately accept his words as God's. First ask yourself these questions:

- What is the person's track record?
- Who is his or her spiritual authority?
- Is the word a confirmation of something God has already put on my heart, or is it something new?
- Does it agree with Scripture?
- What do other people I respect think about this word?
- Does the word inflate my ego, or does it call me to humility?
- Does the person have anything to gain (including prestige and power) if I follow this word?

You may see these questions and assume I'm a negative, cynical person. I'm not, but I've been around long enough to be analytical and cautious. If you ask these questions and the person resents them, that's a huge red flag! Smile, nod, and back away slowly because you're in dangerous territory.

Sometimes the weird people we encounter want to give us a word from God, but sometimes they want a word from us. After I spoke one

Sunday, a lady came up to me and said, "Pastor, I want you to give me a word from the Lord."

I said, "I'm sorry, but I don't have one."

"Sure, you do," she insisted. "You're the pastor."

I handed her my Bible and said, "You're right. I have hundreds of thousands of words from God for you. Here you go."

Circumstances

Be careful when using circumstances to determine God's will. I've heard people say that closed doors and open doors are sure signs of God's directions. I usually feel more certain about the closed doors than the open ones. Let me explain. If you're a high school student you may feel that God is leading you to go to Harvard, but if you have a C average and a low score on your SAT, that door will almost certainly be closed. Sometimes closed doors may only signal "Wait," or perhaps "Try harder" or "Be more creative." But usually the message is, "This isn't the way God is leading you. Ask Him for clear directions."

Similarly, open doors aren't necessarily a sign that God wants us to walk through them. Not every good opportunity is a God opportunity. I have far more open doors than I can possibly walk through. If I pursued every one of them, I would be stretched thin and exhausted, and I would fail at all or most of them.

Actually, I believe that being too dependent on circumstances for direction is a sign of failure to be sensitive to God's voice. Sometimes circumstances "line up" as a secondary, confirming factor, but God's direction is usually more specific and more personal than what we can determine from our circumstances.

When God opens a door, He usually confirms it with some corroborating message: His Word, impressions, the affirmation of others, or something similar. God's message to one of the seven churches in Revelation was, "See, I have placed before you an open door that no one can shut" (Rev. 3:8).

When God opens a door, He usually confirms it with some corroborating message: His Word, impressions, the affirmation of others, or something similar.

Even when God opens a door, we can expect difficulties in accomplishing His purposes. Just as we prune back our plants to help them remain strong and healthy, spiritual pruning (John 15:1–2) is a necessary, though sometimes painful, part of our growth. When we undergo God's pruning, do we interpret it as a closed door? I hope not.

Our perceptions influence how we evaluate our circumstances, resulting in various interpretations. I've heard people say that because they are unhappy in their marriage, God wants them to get a divorce. I've heard people who justified stealing money because a family member left a wallet on the kitchen table. I've heard all kinds of crazy (and selfish) interpretations of "open doors" in people's lives.

God can speak to us through our circumstances, but don't rely on them alone. Look for confirmation from the Scriptures and other sources.

Dreams and Visions

God spoke through dreams to Jacob, Joseph, Pharaoh, Solomon, and Daniel, and He used visions ("waking dreams") to communicate to Abraham, Zachariah, Joseph, Pilate's wife, Cornelius, and Peter. He sometimes still uses those methods to connect with us.

During the most desperate time in her life, Martha Wilson received a vision from God. She explained, "I lost a son who was only six months old. While driving home from the hospital, devastated, I had a vision of Christ holding my son, and I heard Him say, 'Don't worry. He's safe now.'" God's message to Martha didn't make her searing pain go away, but it gave her incredible peace and the courage to walk through her grief.

Today in the Muslim world, God is using dreams and visions of Jesus to convince thousands of people to turn to Him as their Savior. In fact, about one-fourth of those who have converted from Islam to Christianity point to visions and dreams as part of their redemptive experience.[6]

God often gives dreams and visions to point the way forward, but He may also use them to unhook people from the shackles of a painful past. Louis grew up in a chaotic family. He endured verbal and emotional abuse from an alcoholic father and a bitter, overbearing mother. After he became a Christian, his friends sometimes asked him about his background. He told horror stories, but when they asked how all of it had affected him, he just laughed and said, "Oh, I'm fine. It didn't really bother me."

A few years later, however, Louis became clinically depressed. Counselors tried to break through the thick walls of denial and self-protection, but Louis couldn't bring himself to face the painful facts of his life. Without honesty and support, he couldn't grieve and forgive—so he remained stuck as a slave to the festering wounds of his past.

Louis mustered enough strength and courage to move on with his life, but the past slowly poisoned his marriage and his relationship with his two little children. One day as he drove to get ice cream for his son's fourth birthday party, God gave him a vision. Louis saw an angry woman attacking him with a butcher knife. He was terrified and almost ran off the road!

The vision was in silhouette, but as soon as it was over, Louis knew exactly what it meant. It was his mother. She had never come after him with a literal weapon, but he instantly realized her condemnation and demands had cut his soul like a long, sharp knife. From that moment, Louis could no longer deny the reality of his painful past. He began a long healing process and now leads a group for abused and abandoned people. "God broke through that day," he explained years later. "I guess my defenses were so strong that it took a vision from God to begin breaking them down. I'm glad He didn't give up on me."

Visions and dreams may not happen often—and they may never occur for some people—but when they do, God uses them to provide new direction, confirm a word He has already given, or give insight the person desperately needs.

Signs and Wonders

In certain periods of biblical history, God used an unusual number of signs and wonders to confirm His message and His messengers. For example, miracles demonstrated Jesus' divine power and showcased the coming kingdom. God still performs wonders today, often to affirm His love for those who feel abandoned or to confirm His direction for those who are facing challenges.

When Mike Burnette was a college student, he faced a vortex of difficulties that converged at the same time. He was engaged to be married, taking more than a full load of courses so he could graduate on time, performing in three music productions, preparing for his senior recital, and working as the choir director at a church. He had been offered the position of youth pastor at his church, but the thrill of the future was clouded by the pain of the past. Mike had grown up without a father. When the pressures of his life became intense, he began to wonder if the Heavenly Father even cared for him at all. He remembers the night it all became too much to bear:

> On a Sunday night after church, I drove back to campus and parked my car about a mile from my apartment. As I walked across the intramural fields, they were completely dark, and I was all alone. I stood in the middle of the fields and began to pray. It was a time of real desperation for me.
>
> I started to worship God by quoting worship songs. Then I prayed, "God, I want to experience Your presence. Would you shower Your presence on me?"
>
> Immediately, it started raining! I was standing there with my eyes open wide thinking, "THIS IS AMAZING!" Then, as a logical thinker, I wanted to "test and prove" this event. I prayed, "Lord, even if You stop this rain, I'll still believe You're with me."
>
> Immediately, like a sprinkler being turned off, the rain completely stopped. I looked around the field and down the road to see if the rain was moving away, or if it was just a quickly moving shower. Nothing. In fact, when I walked closer to my apartment, the ground wasn't even wet near my building.

No more rain—just me in a field wearing a soaking wet suit and knowing that for that brief moment, God had showered me with His presence. It was just for me, no one else.

That night God didn't speak with words or through His Word. But He spoke louder to me in that moment than ever before. And it changed me. Many times I've doubted the will of God, the plan of God, or even the presence of God, but I often remember that night on the intramural field. God spoke through that shower. I'm still listening.

In close personal relationships, it's perfectly natural to look for confirmations of love. In the same way, God invites us to ask Him for signs of His presence and His direction—especially in the most important decisions in our lives.

Marie was a young woman who wanted to marry Michael, but he only seemed vaguely interested. She felt strongly that God wanted them to marry, but Michael's lack of interest confused and discouraged her. One Sunday morning, Marie prayed, "God, if You're in this, if You want us to be together, have the choir sing 'Holy, Holy, Holy' today in church." That morning when she looked at the program, she saw that the choir was going to sing that song. Marie believed that God had given her a sign from heaven, so she waited patiently for a change in Michael's heart. She didn't have to wait long. He soon became interested in her, and he asked her to marry him a few months later. They've been happily married for two decades. Marie often points back to that Sunday morning as God's assurance that He would fulfill His promise . . . and that a dense young man would get the message!

An Audible Voice

This is the method of divine communication we all want, but it's very rare, even in the Scriptures. God spoke with Adam and Eve before and after they fell into sin; He appeared to Abraham as the angel of the Lord and talked with him; He spoke to the boy Samuel in the temple; He whispered to Elijah when the prophet was depressed; and He spoke at Jesus' baptism, the transfiguration, and just before the crucifixion.

Tamara Holliman isn't a preacher or a pastor. She's incredibly normal—in a good way! At a pivotal moment in her life, God spoke audibly to her. She told me:

> When I was going through my divorce, it was a very significant time in my life and relationship with God. I had done something really stupid . . . which I did a lot of back then. I felt so ashamed and alone. I went on the back porch, crying out to God, just bawling. I wasn't really praying, but I had a repentant heart.
>
> At that moment, I heard an audible voice say "Tamara." I looked around, but no one was there. I put my head back down and cried some more. Again I heard a voice: "Tamara, I love you, My daughter."
>
> That was exactly what I needed to hear—that God still loved me even though I had done all that stupid stuff. It was just amazing.

Robin Applegate had a similar experience in being surprised by the voice of God. In her case, God reminded her that His love was more important than anyone else's.

I never had a date until I was twenty-one. I was saved when I was eleven and filled with the Holy Spirit when I was fifteen. I was very devoted to the Lord and the church. I served the Lord with all my heart. (I was later told that the boys were afraid of me!)

At twenty-one, I started dating a boy, and we thought we were very much in love. He played an instrument in our church band and said he was a Christian. The problem was that he smoked, and when we had a fight, he drank whiskey. I had determined I would never marry a man who smoked or drank. So we had a problem.

I decided to stop seeing him. Immediately, he starting seeing another girl, and a week later they were engaged. I wondered how he could love her when just one week before he had declared his love for me.

One night, I decided I would go to his house and find out.

He lived only two blocks from me. I left my front door and began walking, but as soon as I crossed the street, a voice from heaven as clear as my talking to you said, "You have trusted Me before. Why can't you trust Me now?"

I went as limp as a dishrag. I could hardly walk back to my apartment. I fell on my face and left the matter in God's hands.

LISTEN TO THE KING

The King is worthy of our complete love and loyalty. He isn't just a little bigger and more powerful than we are. He's not a superhero wearing a cape. He's the Creator of all that exists, and His understanding is far beyond anything we can fathom. God has clearly communicated His character, His heart, and His will through His Word. Focus on the Scriptures, and obey what God says through them. If you obey what you read, you'll be more sensitive and receptive to the other ways God can speak to you. Don't look for anything more spectacular than the authoritative, powerful, written Word of God.

The starting point of immediate obedience is the Bible. It's enough, and it's plenty.

CONSIDER THIS . . .

1. Why is it essential to see God as the sovereign, mighty King? What happens to our faith when we see Him as a Santa Claus, a waiter, or a deal maker?

2. Paraphrase this statement: "The key to a thrilling life of being sensitive to the voice of God and immediately obeying Him is the firm belief that God's plan for our lives is fundamentally better than anything we can dream up." Do you believe this is true? Why or why not?

3. If you really believed God was speaking to you through His Word, how excited would you be to read and study it? Where would it fit on your priority list? What would you expect when you opened your Bible and read it?

4. Which of the ways God speaks have you experienced in the last month? In your lifetime?

5. This chapter contains several warnings about people who are manipulative in using "words from God," who listen to poor counsel, and who wrongly interpret circumstances. Which of these do you need to watch out for? Have you been hurt by any of them? If so, explain your answer.

6. Has this chapter inspired you to be open to the various ways God may speak to you? Why or why not?

7. Why is it important to realize the Scriptures are the most spectacular method God uses to communicate with us?

3

WHEN GOD SEEMS SILENT

"To me, faith is a projection into the future. I may not be able to figure out what's going on right now. It may be hard for me to trust God. He may seem far away. But I'm going to go ahead and stake my faith on Him. I'm going to trust Him and believe that one day it will all make sense."
—Philip Yancey

Like most other people on this planet, I easily get distracted by all the pressures of work and life. Sometimes the sense of God's presence and peace is washed away by turmoil, but usually it's not nearly that dramatic. I make a commitment to spend quality time with God, but instead my attention becomes focused on a phone call, an early morning appointment, or a pretty sunrise. It's not vices like drinking, drugs, and gambling that capture my heart. I get distracted by good things: serving the Lord, helping people, preparing messages, hanging out with my family, and other aspects of ministry and home life.

One time I spent three grueling days working on sermons I planned to give months later. Hour after hour, I studied God's Word and tried to craft the messages to have an eternal impact. The first day I felt a little uneasy, but I decided to just press through and keep working. The second day, I still had no sense of peace. I assumed it was a spiritual battle, so I fought hard and stayed focused on the task. Finally, on the third day, the Spirit showed me that I had been working hard *for* God, but not *with* God. There's a difference . . . a huge difference.

When I don't invest regular, quality time with the Lord, His voice becomes distant and faint, and my sense of peace fades away. In those times I become aware that something is missing—*He* seems to be missing—and I need to make some changes in my priorities and my focus.

Busyness isn't a virtue. If your efforts aren't shaped and inspired by the presence of God, they can become a source of pride: "Look at all I'm doing for God!" Or you can resort to self-pity: "Nobody appreciates all I'm doing."

I've noticed that the sense of God's presence and the whisper of His voice vanish when I come to the conclusion that I'm really important. Not long ago I was asked to speak at a major national conference. As the host introduced me, a man behind me leaned forward, put his hand on my shoulder, and said, "Rod, this is your day of advancement." For an instant, I thought, *Yeah! Today, I'm really going to impress these people, and a ton of doors will open for me!* Then God reminded me of an email I had received from a lady in our church only days before. I'm not sure what prompted her to send the message, but I'm glad she did. It basically said, "Pastor Rod, you're nothing. You're just dirt. Sincerely yours," and she signed her name. I had put a copy of her email in the back of the binder holding my talk notes to remind me that my message that day was all about God and not about me.

As I walked to the podium, I realized the man's words enflamed my self-importance, but the woman's prophetic message reminded me that serving God is a gift, a privilege that I should never take for granted. Like Job, I'm nothing but "dust and ashes" (Job 42:6). I sensed God smiling and saying to me, "You're just dirt that I choose to use for My glory. Don't forget that."

TIMES OF SILENCE

I believe it's God's nature to communicate. His book is called "the Word," and His Son is also called "the Word." That's not a mistake or a coincidence. However, God is not on speed dial to give us a message whenever we want one. He's the mysterious and majestic King whose ways are beyond our comprehension. But this King connects with His people . . . unless His people close their ears.

The history of Israel (and the church, for that matter) is a checkered story of glorious faith and colossal failure to trust God. God is incredibly gracious and patient. If He withdrew His presence every time we sinned, we would never hear from Him. After God freed the Israelites from slavery in Egypt and protected them by miraculously parting the Red Sea to let them escape Pharaoh's army, they lacked faith to enter the Promised Land. Even then, God showed His presence in the wilderness with a pillar of fire by night and a cloud by day.

When Solomon built the temple in Jerusalem, the *shekinah* glory of God dwelled in the Holy of Holies in the inner sanctuary. For centuries, through good kings and evil ones, times of trust and times of idolatry, God's presence constantly dwelled in the temple. But finally, when the disobedience of His children became too rampant, God allowed the

Babylonians to destroy the temple. God's people were cast into exile, and the palpable presence of God left them.

When the temple was rebuilt after the exile, the glory of God didn't fill the temple again. The priests were perplexed, but God still spoke to and through the prophets. Their message wasn't always encouraging, but it was always true. God was calling His people to repent and trust Him with their future.

Hundreds of years later, the glory of God finally returned to the temple, but not in a way that anyone expected. It came as two poor young parents arrived with their baby to offer a pauper's sacrifice of two pigeons to consecrate Him. The priests didn't notice, but two faithful old people, Anna and Simeon, realized that God had finally fulfilled His promise to fill the temple again with His glory—the glory of Christ, the Messiah!

The decades after Christ was crucified and resurrected saw the new movement of "the Way" spread throughout the Roman Empire. Ironically, persecution and suffering led to the growth of the church. The most rapid spread of the gospel took place in the second and third centuries when two devastating plagues ravaged the Roman world. Many pagans fled, leaving their sick family members to die. But Christians cared for the diseased unbelievers as well as their own friends and families, and tens of thousands of pagans were so impressed that they became Christians.[7]

When we look back at Israel during the exile, it may have appeared that God was silent, but He had withdrawn the sense of His presence for a purpose: to show people their desperate need for Him. Even then,

He spoke to and through the prophets. And during the persecution and disease of the early centuries of the church, the calamities weren't a result of the sins of the Christians. Their suffering was part of God's grand plan to reach far more people with His love and forgiveness. God was speaking, but His message may have surprised a lot of people.

> God often uses difficulties to get our attention and as fertilizer for our growth.

Don't assume that suffering and setbacks signify God's absence. Actually, God often uses difficulties to get our attention and as fertilizer for our growth. C. S. Lewis observed, "God whispers to us in our pleasures, speaks in our conscience, but shouts in our pains: it is His megaphone to rouse a deaf world."[8]

God wants to talk to us. Whether His message is one of confirmation, comfort, or correction, He is always speaking in and through the Scriptures. We can count on that. Even when we feel spiritually dull, we can remember that Jesus kept teaching and leading a bunch of people who seldom realized who He was. He kept communicating to them, so we can be sure He still communicates with us, too.

However, confusion is the inevitable result whenever we don't hear God speaking to us, so we need to determine the problem. Silence may be an indication of deeper issues: disobedience, distraction, and self-doubt.

Disobedience

People disobey for one of two reasons: ignorance or sin. New believers may simply not know what God wants for them. They haven't read the Bible, they haven't been taught God's will and ways, and they haven't been in a discipleship process that helps them grow.

A sharp young business executive became a Christian, and one of the first messages he heard was that his body is the temple of the Holy Spirit (1 Cor. 6:19–20). His conclusion was to drink only the very best bourbon because he didn't want to dishonor his temple with cheap stuff! (He had some growing to do.)

But ignorance of God's truth isn't usually as laughable. Many people have difficulty separating the truth of the Bible from the philosophies of Deepak Chopra, Dr. Phil, Oprah, and Wayne Dyer. Just before Elijah confronted the prophets of Baal, he told the Israelites they had a choice: "How long will you waver between two opinions? If the LORD is God, follow him; but if Baal is God, follow him" (1 Kings 18:21). Sadly, the people were so conflicted they didn't make a choice—and their failure to choose was a poor choice. Genuine ignorance can be overcome with good teaching and application, but willful ignorance is a different matter. When people *choose* to remain ignorant instead of pursuing God's truth, they've slipped into blatant disobedience.

Truthfully, ignorance isn't usually the real problem at all. The lack of connection with God is the result of a conscious decision to choose something or someone instead of God. In his book, *The Reason for God*, pastor Tim Keller provides a definition of sin:

> "Sin is the despairing refusal to find your deepest identity in your relationship and service to God. Sin is seeking to become

oneself, to get an identity, apart from him. . . . So, according to the Bible, the primary way to define sin is not just the doing of bad things, but the making of good things into *ultimate* things."[9]

For Christians, sin causes a rupture in the lines of communication. Isaiah chided God's people, "But your iniquities have separated you from your God" (Isa. 59:2). People who are married or dating understand this phenomenon. When one person has been selfish, heartless, or irresponsible, the response of the other person is often silence—long, painful silence. The silence is a red flag: "Pay attention! There's a problem here!" Eventually, someone breaks the ice and the ensuing conversation addresses the issue so that forgiveness and understanding mend the relationship.

The same thing can happen in our relationship with God. If He seems silent and distant, it may be an indication that our selfishness has clogged our ears. God is always ready, willing, and able to mend the break, but we have to be honest about our sin.

We can get confused about whether an action or an attitude is sinful. Some people have their consciences "screwed on too tightly" and assume more things are sins than really are. Others have them "screwed on too loosely" and are not aware of blatant sins. The Holy Spirit's job is to clarify truth for us. If we ask, He will show us. Then we can either repent of the sin or take comfort that it wasn't a sin after all.

Most of the time we already know we've sinned. It's not a mystery when we've said hurtful words or committed selfish acts. We just need to be honest about it with God . . . and with the person(s) we've hurt.

At its heart, disobedience is saying no to God. We know what He wants us to be, do, or say, but we ignore it. If we take a minute and think about the truths we recall from God's Word, it doesn't take long for us to see that we're falling short in more than one area. For instance:

- You know what God's Word says about honoring Him with your money, but you spend it on something you want, or save it to feel safe. You're disobedient.

- You know God's standards and desires for relationships, yet you date someone He has said not to date, you go beyond clearly defined sexual boundaries, you're cold and manipulative, or you use words to harm instead of heal. You're disobedient.

- God prompts you to get involved in a ministry, but you make excuses: "I'm too busy," "I'm not good enough," or "They don't need me anyway." Those excuses don't compensate for your disobedience.

- God speaks to you to say something, do something, or give something, but you don't do it. You're disobedient.

- You sense God telling you to stop doing something, but you keep doing it. You promise you'll stop . . . sometime. Delay is disobedience.

Sin isn't an accident. Active, intentional disobedience quiets the voice of God in your life. God is still speaking, but your disobedience creates a barrier of spiritual deafness. If you want to hear from God, go back to your latest point of disobedience, and repent. Write the check. Share your faith. Stop the habit. Break up. Do whatever God told you to do.

Then, just listen. You'll begin to hear God speak again. The principle is clear: God won't give you the *next* word until you obey His *last* word.

> God won't give you the *next* word until you obey His *last* word.

Distractions

Have you noticed that being distracted often makes us irritable? We try so hard but either don't make progress or don't get appreciated—or both. As I have said, it's easy to be distracted from God even by the good and important things we do. The solution isn't to become a monk, but to rearrange our priorities and live by them rigorously.

When Jesus went to the home of His friends, Mary sat as His feet to listen while Martha cooked dinner. Martha wasn't too happy about being left alone in the kitchen. I can imagine her coming into the living room in her apron and putting her hands on her hips as she barked at Jesus, "Lord, don't you care that my sister has left me to do the work by myself? Tell her to help me!"

Jesus tenderly replied, "Martha, Martha, you are worried and upset about many things, but few things are needed—or indeed only one. Mary has chosen what is better, and it will not be taken away from her" (Luke 10:41–42).

We can't eliminate all the pressures and voices that clamor for our attention, but we can learn to say no to at least some of those things in order to carve out time with God and make sure we hear His voice. We also need to realize that some seasons of life are simply tougher than others. Mothers of young children can't turn them off like an appliance, and the incessant voices of children can easily drown out the voice of God. I want to say to those mothers, "You have the most distracting, demanding job in the world. You need twenty minutes in a hot tub every day. You might fall asleep there, but I trust God will speak to you in your sleep!" And some jobs require sixty or seventy hours a week for periods of time. Even then—*especially* then—we need to make sure we rivet our hearts to the Lord and draw on the vast resources of His love, wisdom, and strength.

Self-Doubt

I've talked to people who've been taught that God promises to speak so they can obey, but they conclude that they're disqualified from such a dynamic relationship. They fully believe God speaks to other people, but not to them. They may have committed some sin so awful that it haunts them, or they may have been crushed in a relationship with a parent or spouse. For whatever reason, they can't imagine anyone in authority—especially God—will ever love them, forgive them, and want them.

Others conclude that God speaks to pastors and missionaries, but not to ordinary people. They shrug and say, "I'm just a run of the mill, average person. What would God want with someone like me?"

Self-doubt is, to be sure, a real problem for some people. Those who are deeply wounded need comfort, assurance, and healing. But people who want to excuse themselves for being average just need to be challenged. The Bible says that no one is beyond the grace of God. All who have been adopted into His family are commissioned to represent Him to the world! God has given you a new identity as a chosen, adopted, forgiven, empowered, directed child of the King!

Peter described our new identity this way, "But you are a chosen people, a royal priesthood, a holy nation, God's special possession, that you may declare the praises of him who called you out of darkness into his wonderful light" (1 Peter 2:9).

You are qualified, not by your intelligence, looks, résumé, skills, or personality, but by the payment Christ made to rescue you from darkness and make you His own. Believe it. Bathe in it. And live by it.

WHAT'S THE PROBLEM?

When God seems silent, the problem isn't that He is distant or dead. The problem is that disobedience, distractions, and/or self-doubt have plugged our ears so that we don't hear what He's saying to us.

I saw a vivid (and humorous) illustration of this one night at church when one of our pastors, Gary, made announcements. I was sitting on the front row, but I could barely hear him. Kids were crying and talking, and their parents were trying to get them to be quiet . . . by talking really loudly! I looked around to watch the show. Gary was talking loudly enough, but no one was listening. He could have been announcing, "Next Sunday the apostle Paul is going to be our special guest. He will autograph the book of Romans in your Bible immediately following third service. By the way, the President and his family will be with us next Sunday. He watches online every week. And I have $1,000 for anyone who will come up front right now."

I felt bad for Gary, even though I was amused by the spectacle. But it's not funny when we treat God like Pastor Gary. Whenever God speaks, He has something worthwhile to say, and if we're completely checked out and paying absolutely no attention, we stand to miss out on important things. God is constantly speaking: guiding, directing, and leading.

I get frustrated when I talk to people who don't listen. Cindy is a wonderful wife, but sometimes she doesn't listen very well. She'll ask me a question, and I'll answer. Two hours later, she asks again. The next morning, she doesn't remember our conversation so she asks the same question a third time. On the rare occasions when this happens, I sometimes tell her, "Cindy, I don't think you're paying attention to me. I answered your question twice last night. Don't you remember?" I wonder if God ever gets frustrated that He's talking but we aren't listening?

Some people don't listen for God's voice because they don't want to hear what He has to say. Oh, they've got a pretty good idea what He might say, but they're comfortable and don't want to change. Or they're disobedient, and they don't want to be corrected. They don't want to hear Him say, "Stop it," or "Give this," or "Change that." They don't want to hear Him calling them to do something or say something out of their comfort zone. To avoid an instruction that makes them uncomfortable, they simply refuse to listen . . . and then complain that God isn't speaking to them!

Think about kids and their parents. A mom or dad can whisper, "Hey, do you want some money?" The kid hears that message and comes running. But the parents can shout, "Clean your room" a dozen times and never be heard. Why? The children don't *want* to hear it. It's an instruction they don't enjoy, so they intentionally ignore their parents' voices.

God is patient and persistent, but if we ignore Him too long, our hearts become insensitive and unresponsive, like leather instead of supple skin.

Ignoring God's voice is serious business. God is patient and persistent, but if we ignore Him too long, our hearts become insensitive and unresponsive, like leather instead of supple skin. The writer to the Hebrews warns:

> "See to it, brothers and sisters, that none of you has a sinful, unbelieving heart that turns away from the living God. But encourage one another daily, as long as it is called 'Today,' so that none of you may be hardened by sin's deceitfulness. We have come to share in Christ, if indeed we hold our original conviction firmly to the very end. As has just been said: 'Today, if you hear his voice, do not harden your hearts as you did in the rebellion'" (Heb. 3:12–15).

Sadly, many people have been in church for a number of years and have heard countless sermons about the vitality of God's engagement with people, but they haven't made the connection to their own lives. They simply don't expect to hear God's voice. It's not that they can't hear Him, and it's certainly not that He isn't speaking to them. The problem is that they read the Bible as a textbook on history and theology instead of a love letter written personally to them, and their prayer is a one-way street. They make plenty of requests, but they have no expectation that God might want to say something to them as they pray.

NEVER DISAPPOINTED

I expect God to speak to me. I'm always listening for His voice. Because I'm listening for it, I'm more likely to hear it. When I hear Him, I'm never disappointed. His message may be wonderfully affirming, and I love to hear it, or it may scare me to death—either way, it's a thrill.

Even when the people of Israel were at their worst and had been taken into exile, God promised to reveal Himself to them. Through Jeremiah, God assured them:

> "This is what the LORD says: 'When seventy years are completed for Babylon, I will come to you and fulfill my good promise to bring you back to this place. For I know the plans I have for you,' declares the LORD, 'plans to prosper you and not to harm you, plans to give you hope and a future. Then you will call on me and come and pray to me, and I will listen to you. You will seek me and find me when you seek me with all your heart. I will be found by you,' declares the LORD, 'and will bring you back from captivity. I will gather you from all the nations and places where I have banished you,' declares the LORD, 'and will bring you back to the place from which I carried you into exile'" (Jer. 29:10–14).

That's God's promise: If we seek Him, we'll find Him; if we listen, we'll hear His voice (Matt. 7:7–8). If God was willing to be found by His wayward people centuries ago, surely He wants us to hear, find, and obey Him today.

When you listen for God's voice, sooner or later you'll hear Him. It's a matter of focus. It's like when you decide you might want to buy a particular model of car, you suddenly start seeing that kind of car far more often than before. When your focus changes, your receptivity increases exponentially.

Or suppose as a New Year's resolution, you decide to get in shape. You've never run before, but you make a commitment to run several miles four times a week. You buy the clothes, read the magazines, and join a club with a track. Instinctively, you begin to notice other people wearing running clothes and looking fit. As you watch them, you analyze their technique. You take note of the shoes of the person sitting across from you at a restaurant, and you conclude he must be a runner. Those people had been around you all along, but you didn't see them because you weren't looking for them. When your focus changed, your perception changed.

In elementary school, boys think girls are yucky and girls think boys are stupid. Ask a young guy if there are cute girls in his class, and he will exclaim, "Absolutely not!" Ask a girl if she likes any boys, and she says, "No way!" Then, at about sixth or seventh grade, something called puberty happens. Hormones kick in. Suddenly boys begin to notice girls, and girls can't stop talking about boys. And other things change: they start wearing deodorant, shaving or wearing makeup, taking showers, and insisting on cute clothes. What happened? Their focus changed, and they started noticing people who had been in their classes for years.

One more example: Before iPods, and even before CD players, I used to have a little green radio. I loved that radio. It was not digital, so it had a tuning dial. It was hard to get the right frequency for some of the stations, so as I carefully turned the dial I would hear static . . . and more static . . . until suddenly my rock and roll station would blare my favorite songs! The music was there all along. It was in the air all around me, ready to be heard. All I had to do was tune in to the right place on the dial so I could hear it.

> When you start actively listening for the voice of God—when you're tuning in to God's frequency—you're much more likely to hear Him!

Here's the connection: When you start actively listening for the voice of God—when you're tuning in to God's frequency—you're much more likely to hear Him! He's speaking. You just haven't been listening for the tone of His voice. When you start listening, you'll discover just how much He speaks.

When I presented this concept to our church, several people looked sheepish the first week. I asked them what they were thinking, and they all said something like, "Uh, what if I listen but I don't hear anything from God?" I assured them they could rely on God's promise to speak to them. After they began tuning their ears to listen, no one came back with a report that they hadn't heard anything from God.

But there are no guarantees, no formulas, and no rituals that will guarantee a voice will come at any given time. It's a relationship, not a computer program. God speaks *when* He wants, *how* He wants, and *what* He wants.

Anyone who predicts how often God will speak is manipulative and arrogant . . . or maybe just foolish. We're not in a competition to be able to say we've heard God speak more often and more dramatically than someone else. And we don't need to make superstars out of people who claim to hear God's voice. When we're amazed at a person instead of amazed at God, we're completely missing the focus of where the glory should reside. We don't become sensitive to God in an attempt to keep score and win. It's human nature to be competitive—*fallen* human nature! *We're* not special because we hear His voice; *He* is special because He is so kind to communicate with us. God will speak what you need to hear when you need to hear it in a way you can understand. It's different for each person, but I guarantee that He will speak because He is true to His promises.

GETTING CONNECTED

I've talked to plenty of people who wondered why they didn't hear from God, but after a few minutes of conversation the reason became abundantly clear: they had never become God's children. Some had followed rules all their lives and hoped that was good enough to get them into heaven, and others assumed God would grade on a curve when they died. Since they weren't any worse than most people they knew, they assumed they were above the cutoff point. That's not the gospel of grace.

Let me use an illustration from my own life. I have a gift for getting lost. I can barely find my way back from the bathroom without a map. Even with a map, I get turned around and go in the wrong direction. I've been lost on three continents and in dozens of countries. Cindy used to marvel when I called to announce that I had arrived at the right city, and even more if I had found the right hotel.

But a few years ago my sense of direction underwent a fantastic transformation when someone gave me a GPS system. I was a new man, always on the right path thanks to constant contact with a source that guided me. Oh, there have been plenty of times when I've heard that grating word: "Recalculating." But with corrections, I was soon back on track.

Those who are spiritually lost need God to become their GPS. They can't manufacture one on their own; the only way to get it is to receive it as a gift. To receive it, we have to accept the bad news and the good news. The bad news is that we are so sinful (even those who have tried so hard to earn God's approval) that it took the death of the Son of God to pay for our sins. The Bible says that apart from the grace of Christ, we are hopeless and helpless, enemies of God and dead to Him.

But the good news is that God loves us unconditionally, and His Son was glad to lay down His life for us. When we accept Christ's payment on the cross for our sins, incredible things happen. All our sins are forgiven—past, present, and future. God declares believers righteous in His eyes, not because they have earned it by being good enough, but because Jesus earned it by living a perfect life.

We count on His righteousness, not ours. But that's not all. God not only rescued us from sin and death; He also adopted us as His own children. He embraces us as His dearly loved sons and daughters, and we have the kind of relationship with Him that a loved child has with a wise and loving parent. We call Him "Abba" (Daddy).

This incredible reality brings us back to the fact that our Abba is the King of glory, the Creator of all and the One who longs to speak words of comfort, correction, and direction to us. We don't have to twist His arm to get Him to communicate with us. That's His nature. We just have to get on the same wavelength, and we get there by faith in His sheer grace.

If you've been on the outside looking in, if you realize you've been trying to impress God by following rules, or if you've assumed God would grade on a curve but now you realize sin is serious business, you can do something about it. If your family is in turmoil, your life has lost its purpose, and you don't know where to turn, there's hope in the arms of God. No one is too lost for God to find and forgive. No one is too sinful to be cleansed by Jesus' blood.

Prayer is talking with God. In your own words, or using mine, express your heart to God. Accept His wondrous grace, and know that you're connected to Him.

Lord Jesus, I've been running my own life, and it hasn't worked. I need You. I admit that I'm a sinner, and I thank You for forgiving me. I want to know You, love You, and follow You. Be the King of my hopes, my habits, my finances, my family, and every other part of my life. I give You everything I am and everything I have. I'm all Yours. Change me from the inside out, and make me sensitive to hear Your voice. Amen.

Christians—those who trust Christ as their Savior at some point in their lives—may feel lost and disconnected from God if they hold something back from Him. They may allow Him to be Lord of their job, but not their finances; of their habits, but not a special relationship. When we lock God out of a part of our lives, the cancer of unbelief and resistance grows. God keeps whispering to invite us to come back to Him, but we tune Him out.

If that's the case with you, don't wait a minute longer. If the Holy Spirit is shining the light of conviction on an area (or two) of your life, be honest with God. Confess your sin and accept God's forgiveness, strength, and new direction. Invite Him to be the King of every area of your life.

It's never the wrong time to be genuine with God. It's always the right time to embrace Him and let Him embrace you. Don't waste another hour living in confusion, resentment, and aimlessness. God is speaking to you. Will you answer?

FRESH HOPE

Randall Young felt desperate and discouraged. He had asked God to answer a prayer so many times he had lost count. When the answer didn't come, he assumed God had abandoned him. But in his despair, God showed up. This is the letter Randall sent me:

Pastor Rod:

A few weeks ago you announced the opening of the Hot Springs Village Church. That Sunday afternoon I felt God start to deal with me about going to this new work. In my mind, I had a list of reasons why I couldn't go!

As you know, this last year and a half has tested my faith. Through it all, I did my best to keep a smile on my face and not show how deeply hurt I truly was. I have spoken about faith, and that God will answer prayer, but I found myself on my knees crying out to God. I felt defeated, beat down, embarrassed, humiliated. I found myself a lot of Friday nights alone in our sanctuary praying for God to restore my family. Pastor, that prayer was not answered.

After the Sunday you spoke about Hot Springs, God started dealing with me—night and day, day and night. I kept telling myself, "There's no way Pastor Rod would even want me." But when I listened to your first sermon on immediate obedience, it was hitting me hard. Pastor, God showed me I'm called to serve. Every word you spoke was directly to me. I had felt so defeated, but I know when God is dealing with me.

I walked into that meeting for Hot Springs without a clue if I would be accepted to serve, but as soon as I arrived, you walked over and said, "Randall, I was hoping you'd come!" I broke down in tears. You don't have a clue what those words meant to me. A load was lifted off my shoulders. I'll serve with everything I have, and our work in Hot Springs will bear fruit.

As I walked out of that meeting, Pastor Tim walked over and put his arms around my neck. He told me that he had watched me during the sermon on immediate obedience, and he knew God was working on me. God let him know I was going to Hot Springs. He said he was so proud that I had answered God's calling.

Pastor Rod, thank you for allowing me to serve.

Randall

CONSIDER THIS . . .

1. Do you agree or disagree with the assumption that God is always speaking to you? Explain your answer.

2. How would you define sin?

3. How does sin cloud or crush the lines of communication between God and you?

4. In the last week or two, what are some distractions that have taken you away (or threatened to take you away) from quality time with God?

5. What are some self-doubts people may have that make them feel disqualified from hearing God? Do any of those ring true in your mind and heart?

6. How is learning to listen to God like tuning an analog radio?

7. In getting and staying connected with God, why is it important to let Him be King of every area of your life?

4

THE PROOF OF OUR LOVE

"God's heart is the most sensitive and tender of all.
No act goes unnoticed, no matter how insignificant or small."
—Richard Foster

All love is sacrificial. In every aspect of life, expressions of devotion and loyalty come at a price. Soldiers sacrifice for their comrades and their country. Parents endure sleepless nights, wiping up messes, reading stories, spending a small fortune, and many years of attention for kids who give back little in return. Lovers and spouses give up time and conveniences for one another. Friends bend over backwards to help each other. In each case, the sacrifice is made willingly because of the person's strong love.

Of course, the ultimate expression of sacrificial love is the incarnation, life, and death of Jesus Christ. He lived in matchless glory in perfect fellowship with the Father and the Spirit, but He put that aside to rescue hopeless, helpless sinners. As the wonder of God's amazing love penetrates our hearts, we will love Him in return and want to please Him in every way possible. In short, we will obey out of hearts overflowing with gratitude.

After Jesus ate His last meal with His disciples, He took them out on a hillside for some final encouragement, warnings, and instructions. They had been with Him for more than three years. They had seen His exquisite tenderness with the poor, the sick, outcasts, and those who were crushed by guilt. And they had watched as He fiercely defended truth against the attacks and sanctimony of the religious leaders. Through it all, they noticed His unwavering devotion to the Father. Jesus' loyalty had been demonstrated in countless ways, but it was about to be shown most dramatically in His obedience to undergo His supreme purpose: to give His life as a ransom for us.

That last night together, Jesus asked His followers to have the same devotion—to let their love inspire obedience. In fact, this message was so important, Jesus said it twice:

> "If you love me, keep my commands. . . . Whoever has my commands and keeps them is the one who loves me. The one who loves me will be loved by my Father, and I too will love them and show myself to them" (John 14:15, 21).

We can summarize Jesus' statements in two different ways. In a positive sense, if we love Him, we will obey Him because we want to. But from another perspective, if we don't obey Him, it proves we don't really love Him. Obedience is the rock-solid proof of our love for Jesus.

Many times we are quick with excuses when we sense God nudging us, which is why I believe we need to make a commitment to obey *immediately*. Sometimes when we resist, God gives us a second chance (like with Jonah). But other times the moment is fleeting and gone in an instant.

Once when I attended a conference, I stayed on the tenth floor of a hotel. As I waited for the elevator, I overheard two of the house-keeping staff in the hallway discussing the hassles they had faced earlier that morning. One of them had been pressured to get her work done more quickly, and the other had been late because she got stuck in traf-fic driving her daughter to school. I sensed God tell me to give them each $100. I had the money in my wallet, but I hesitated. I wondered, *Is this from God or is it just my idea?* After a few seconds, the elevator arrived. I got on and left them in the tenth floor hallway.

By the time the elevator got to the lobby, I was thinking, *How could I be so stupid? What difference does it make if this was a "God thought" or a "Rod thought"? Either way, it would have been a kind thing to do.* I imme-diately turned around, hit the elevator button, and went back to my floor. When the doors opened, the women were gone. I walked down the halls to try to find them, but they had left the floor. I regretted that I had missed an opportunity to be a blessing to them.

Five months later, I attended another event in the city and stayed at the same hotel. When I got off the elevator on my floor, I saw a house-keeper—one of the two ladies I had overheard! But I was stuck behind some others in the hall and she vanished around a corner before I could say anything. I missed her again.

After I went to bed that evening I woke up in the middle of the night. It didn't take a genius to figure out what God was saying to me.

I knew He was going to let our paths cross one more time so I could give her the money and tell her it was from Jesus.

The next morning I told Cindy the whole story and then said: "Today's the day. You and I are going to find her. I was supposed to give her some money five months ago, but I was disobedient. I don't know what happened to the other lady, but I know this one still works at the hotel. This time, I'm going to do it."

We got dressed and left the room to have breakfast. The lady was pushing her cart only a few doors down. I pulled the money out of my wallet and explained, "I'm working on being immediately obedient when God tells me to do something. I sensed God tell me to give this to you. This isn't from me. It's from God. He also asked me to tell you something: He knows where you are and knows what you need." I handed her the $100.

She immediately broke down in tears. She thanked us over and over again. It was obvious this was about much more than the money. A simple act of kindness had touched her deeply. Cindy and I hugged her. I said, "Don't thank us. Thank God. He is giving this to you. He's just giving it through us."

I felt equal parts of thrill and relief. It was heartwarming to see God use us in that way, and I had finally closed the loop on being obedient to God. But that's not the end of the story. The next day, I received an email forwarded to me from the hotel sales manager. It read:

> *Wow.*
>
> *We were all touched this morning by the action of a guest of the AOG Executive Presbytery. The guest had a Do Not Disturb sign on his door during his stay, so his room was not serviced by*

a housekeeper. However, yesterday he approached a housekeeper, Beth, and told her that the Lord spoke to him and told him to take care of her. He handed her $100.

Beth is a single mother of a young daughter. She is a very hard worker and does an excellent job. She was blown away by his generosity and is using the money to provide Christmas gifts for her daughter.

Below is a picture of Beth from our Facebook page. Several months ago she was named a Service Champion because of how she attends to our guests by writing them notes as well as noticing and taking care of their preferences. However, she had not serviced the guest's room, so she was truly blown away by his gift.

I wanted to let you know we all enjoyed hearing about this. What a special person. We are so glad to be of service to you and your guests, and we appreciate how you treat us.

Doris Keeting

I wish I had been obedient five months earlier. I'm sure God met her need some other way at that time because He is not dependent on us. But when we fail to respond in faith, we miss the blessing. Even when our obedience is delayed or flawed, God uses us to touch hearts and change lives. Our willingness to obey is the daily, uncomplicated proof of our love for Christ. It's the acid test of what (and who) really matters to us.

> Our willingness to obey is the daily, uncomplicated proof of our love for Christ.

ALL OF US ARE SLAVES

Slaves? Why are we discussing that issue in a book in the twenty-first century? Didn't we fight a war about that a century and a half ago? Yes, but there are many different kinds of slavery.

Addiction, to a substance or a behavior, is an easy type of slavery to identify. But we can also be slaves to work, a person's approval, career, television, money, our kids, Facebook, clothes, a favorite sports team, or almost anything else. We are slaves to any master that controls our behavior and captures our minds, goals, and money. We're slaves to anything that commands our affections and robs us of choices.

In chattel slavery during the eighteenth and nineteenth centuries in America, masters demanded a slave's obedience and unquestioning compliance in everything: time, money, attention, and devotion. The slaves didn't set their priorities; the master did.

In his letter to the Romans, Paul made a distinction between race-based permanent slavery and the kind that is pervasive in humanity: "Don't you know that when you offer yourselves to someone as obedient slaves, you are slaves of the one you obey—whether you are slaves to sin, which leads to death, or to obedience, which leads to righteousness?" (Rom. 6:16)

Slavery may seem to be a foreign concept in a modern democracy, but the fact is that every person is a slave of something or someone. However, unlike the slavery of the American South and other parts of the world, we have a *choice* of masters. We will obey something or someone. We can be slaves of sin (in any of its many forms), or we can make God our Lord and Master. If your first priority is the pursuit of anything other than God, you are a slave to whatever that is.

Only one Master is worthy of our complete loyalty and obedience. We need to choose the Master who is infinitely loving, wise, and strong. All the others promise fulfillment, order, and thrills, but they eventually leave us empty, broken, and alone.

OBEDIENCE IS A LEARNED BEHAVIOR

No one has to convince a parent that a child's obedience is learned (or not learned) over time. The home is a hothouse for a child's development, and one of the most important aspects of growth is learning to obey the parents. In the same way, we need to learn how to respond to God so that obedience becomes instinctive and reflexive. The more we trust someone, the more willing we are to do what he or she instructs. This kind of instant trust doesn't develop overnight. It takes time, encouragement, correction, and plenty of repentance when we fail.

Amazingly, even Jesus had to learn this lesson. The writer to the Hebrews tells us,

> "During the days of Jesus' life on earth, he offered up prayers and petitions with fervent cries and tears to the one who could save him from death, and he was heard because of his reverent submission. . Son though he was, he learned obedience from what he suffered and, once made perfect, he became the source of eternal salvation for all who obey him" (Heb. 5:7–9).

Two points stand out in this passage. First, if the perfect, sinless Son of God had to learn to be obedient, we shouldn't be surprised when it takes a process for us to learn to obey God, too. This passage certainly doesn't imply that Jesus was ever disobedient. But in His experience as a human being, He encountered the choices all of us face. And as Jesus "grew in wisdom and stature" (Luke 2:52), He chose at every moment to trust the Father and obey Him.

Second, the classroom where Jesus learned about obedience was His suffering. When Satan tempted Him in the wilderness, when He encountered opposition, when most of His closest friends deserted Him, and even when He faced the horror of the cross, Jesus obeyed the Father. Through it all, He kept obeying "for the joy set before him" (Heb. 12:2)—the joy of bringing hopeless sinners into the family of God. We should see from His example that suffering always has a far greater payoff than we can imagine, sometimes here on earth, and certainly when we see Him face to face.

The promise of ultimate joy allows me to reinterpret suffering. I don't have to second-guess myself, and I have the assurance that God will, in fact, work all things together for good for those who trust Him. I can sleep well at night because I know I've listened to the Father's voice and responded in faith. With this assurance, I can be a little more like Jesus: I can welcome suffering so that I learn obedience, too.

I'm afraid many Christians don't understand that suffering is God's classroom to teach us life's most important lessons. Some pastors and teachers even promise just the opposite: that God will make their lives problem-free and pleasant. It would appear that those folks haven't read much of the Bible! Jesus told His followers, "In this world you will have trouble." That's His promise! Then He explained, "But take heart! I have overcome the world" (John 16:33).

No one likes to suffer, but it's part of God's curriculum for all of us to deepen our faith, take the rough edges off our character, and give us compassion for others in pain. Through experiences of heartache, difficulty, and rejection, we learn to obey for very different reasons than just to be blessed. We obey because we want to be as close to God as possible during hard times, and we want God to reach through our pain to refine us, sharpen us, and deepen our dependence on Him.

You're going to experience pain. Don't waste it. Learn obedience through it.

You're going to experience pain. Don't waste it. Learn obedience through it.

This insight took a lot of weight off my shoulders. For a while I felt guilty because I struggled to be more obedient to God. But if Jesus needed to learn obedience, I could give myself a little grace and realize there's a learning curve. I won't get it right every time, but as I practice listening and obeying, I'll get better at it. Like any habit, obedience becomes more intuitive as we do it more regularly. But it's more than a habit. Just as enslavement to a person or behavior leads to deeper entanglement, obedience to God leads to deeper devotion to Him. The difference is that one kind of slavery crushes and kills, but willing and immediate obedience to God increasingly produces joy, life, and light.

I'm not sure about a lot of things, but I'm certain about this: if people practice listening to God and immediately obeying for ninety days, they won't say, "That was cool, but now I'm done. I'm going back to doing everything my way because it was so much more fulfilling." As they start the 90-day trial, they will have many fits and starts, ups and downs, hits and misses. But after just two or three weeks they will realize they have discovered a new and better way to live. When that happens, they won't ever want to go back.

When we blow it (and we will), we don't have to kick ourselves or give up in despair. We can be honest with God and determine to do better next time. And sometimes, the next time happens really quickly.

A couple of years ago I was flying home from Spokane, Washington, where I had spoken at a banquet. When I walked to the gate for my flight, a young lady standing nearby asked me, "How can you tell when to board the plane?"

She showed me her boarding pass, and I pointed to the boarding group number in the corner, smiled, and said, "That's a pretty good clue." She laughed, and we introduced ourselves. Her name was Brittany.

Neither of us was in a hurry, so we talked for a few minutes. She asked me what I was doing, and I told her I had spoken at a banquet to raise money to buy Bibles for people who couldn't afford them. She looked happily surprised and told me, "That's really cool. I went to church yesterday . . . for the first time in a long time." We talked a few more minutes, and then it was time to board.

When I got on the plane, I completely forgot about Brittany. I was engrossed in going over my talk and reading a magazine. When we arrived in Denver, where I was making a connection, I met some friends and we went to a restaurant in the airport. But as soon as we sat down, the Lord reminded me of the young lady. I told the guys, "Hey, I had a God assignment, but I missed it. I need to see if I can find someone God put in my path and talk to her about Him. I may not be back anytime soon. You go ahead and eat."

When Brittany and I had talked in Spokane, she had told me her final destination. In Denver, I checked the flight monitors and I guessed where she would make her connection. I walked to that gate and waited for a while until I saw her walk up. She was surprised to see me again. I'm not sure if people nearby thought I was a stalker or a pervert preying on pretty young women, but I didn't worry about that. I was on a mission.

I said, "Brittany, I've been looking for you. I wanted to talk with you a little more. You said you went to church yesterday. Tell me about that."

We sat down together, and she pulled a notebook out of her backpack. She had taken notes of the sermon. I immediately realized the pastor had used the same passage I had prepared for the banquet. As if I needed confirmation that this was a "God moment," I had it! As we talked, she told me her life had been spinning out of control. Her best friend had died tragically, she had lost her job, and she was moving to a city where she didn't know anyone. In her despair and confusion, she had reached out to God by walking into a church service the day before.

As we talked, we heard the first boarding call for her flight—and the second, and the third. We heard the announcement that they were ready to close the doors. I asked Brittany if I could pray for her. I took her hand, we prayed for God to show himself to her in remarkable ways, and I thanked Him for letting me have this time with her. As she walked through the doors to the plane, tears streamed down my face. I prayed, "Lord, thank You for giving me another chance. I'm so glad I didn't miss this moment with Brittany." And I prayed what has become a common prayer for me, "Lord, please give me another chance every time I fail to hear Your voice or fail to respond when I do."

TOO SMALL?

When we read the Bible or listen to missionaries speak, we may get the impression that hearing and obeying God is always about monumental events: confronting Pharaoh, killing Goliath, surviving lions' dens or fiery furnaces, walking on water, seeing thousands reached with the gospel, healing desperately ill people, and other awe-inspiring activities that make us say, "Wow!"

However, if we expect God to give us only big tasks like those, we'll be disappointed. He asks us to obey Him in the little things. The measure of our love for God isn't when we say yes to stand for Jesus in front of hundreds or thousands, but to obey when no one is looking. In truth, someone is always looking. God notices, He cares, and He smiles when we are more concerned about honoring Him than being seen by others.

Tina learned this lesson, and it made all the difference in the world.

Pastor Rod,

I'm inspired by those I consider heroes of faith when I hear their stories of following God's leading even when they felt the task was too large and their qualifications too small. Many have dared to risk their lives, their comfort, and their reputations by pursuing what looked to be impossible—but they obeyed anyway, and God brought them incredible victories. When I think of obedience, those are the stories I want to hear. I love those stories.

Last year I really yearned to be more involved in some sort of service to our church. I began to pray earnestly that God would lead me to a ministry where I could use my gifts to change lives— and be able to tell a great story of my obedience.

As I prayed, God led me to a particular area of service, but I didn't immediately pursue it. The reason why I didn't is the reason why I felt I should share this with you. I've read many books and heard lots of teaching on how to trust God and obey His prompt- ings when the act of obedience seems insurmountable, ill-advised, or impossible. Doing something great—that's what I wanted . . . that's what I expected. But that's not what God was telling me to do. It was only one thing, and it wasn't a big thing.

I knew what God wanted me to do, but I kept rationalizing that anyone could do it. Surely He must have something else in mind for me! I'm embarrassed to admit it, but I thought about my qualifications: I had graduated from college with an MA in educa- tion. I love to create. I love to interact with people. I love to teach. I love to think and wrestle with complicated concepts. The thing God was asking me to do seemed, well, beneath me. I wanted God to give me a task I was uniquely qualified to do, something that stretched me and required faith and courage. I wanted an Esther story. I wanted to someone to say about me: "And who knows but that you have come to your royal position for such a time as this?" but God's direction wasn't very royal. Actually, it wasn't even a position. It was a mundane assignment . . . something that would bore me. It didn't require courage, or big dreams, or huge leaps of faith, or the promise of doing something great for God that would change the world. It only required one thing . . . obedience.

Just obedience.

Sometimes "just obedience" is much harder than it sounds. It's hard to glamorize it. It doesn't preach well in a sermon. Or read well in a book. But I bet I'm not the only person who has struggled to obey God's leading because the task seemed too small . . . too common. When all God requires of you is obedience to do something that isn't spectacular, it's easy to dismiss it and wait until He hands out the big stuff.

I wasted time waiting for God to lead me to something else, but eventually I pursued this area of ministry. Now I love to serve every Tuesday at the Membership Services building. And I love it! I wanted to do this to be of service to my church, but God turned it into something that ministers to me. This result was totally unexpected. Each Tuesday when I leave I'm still surprised by what that day has given me. I tell my husband it's my therapy.

Tina

The proof of our love is our willingness—even eagerness—to obey God when no one applauds, and when no one even notices . . . when it's "just obedience."

BLESSING FOLLOWS OBEDIENCE

Spiritual life isn't a vending machine. It's not just about laws and rules. We have a Father who loves us, cheers us on, and delights to bless us when we respond to Him with faith, hope, and love. Parents are like that. They can't wait to bless their responsive kids. Jesus made this point in His most famous sermon: "Which of you, if your son asks for bread, will give him a stone? Or if he asks for a fish, will give him a snake? If you, then, though you are evil, know how to give good gifts to your children, how much more will your Father in heaven give good gifts to those who ask him!" (Matt. 7:9–11)

Good parents understand that blessing disobedient kids only reinforces their selfishness. If a mom smiles and cheers while her toddler plays in the street, he's going to do it again and again. Or if parents turn a blind eye and give tacit approval to drug use, lying, or sexual promiscuity, the kids make the logical conclusion that the behavior is perfectly acceptable. God is a perfect parent, and He never gives His children wrong signals. We're foolish if we get upset with Him for not blessing us when we're disobedient.

This principle isn't just a spiritual one. Employers reward workers who are responsible and obedient. Schools give awards to students who show discipline and effort, not those who could care less about learning. The difference is that God, in His grace, will forgive disobedience. This fact shouldn't make us complacent. Instead, it ought to amaze us and motivate us to love and obey Him more.

We may experience times of pruning and suffering, but even then, God longs to bless us with His presence and assure us that we're in the center of His will. The best and safest place is right in the center of God's purposes and paths.

Disobedience opens us to all kinds of dangers. Even when we don't understand the reasons God is telling us to do something, it's safer to do it than to say, "No, I'd rather not." When we respond to God in faith, we put ourselves under His umbrella of blessing and protection. But when we ignore or reject God's leading, we expose ourselves more fully to the evil forces of the world, the flesh, and the devil. Immediate obedience keeps us intimately connected to His heart and on board with His plans for us.

> Immediate obedience keeps us intimately connected to His heart and on board with His plans for us.

If we will listen—patiently and persistently—God will use even our biggest heartaches to bless us and others. Unwanted suffering seems to be the exact opposite of God's blessing, but it's often the unexpected door to a closer relationship with God and a more profound impact on others.

Robin Tolliver anticipated her child's birth with eagerness, but she and her husband Seth were stunned with the doctor's announcement of their baby's physical condition. Still, they never gave up on God. Robin explains:

Pastor,

Presley was diagnosed with Down syndrome shortly after her birth. I began reading, researching, and learning everything I could about her diagnosis—what we could do to help her, what she needed nutritionally, why everyone kept saying to get her into therapy immediately, and how to navigate through the government system called "Early Intervention."

I diligently wrote everything down throughout this process. I was surprised how confusing and difficult it was. I was told by the social worker to just take her home, accept her as she was, and mourn for the child I didn't get. Doctors told me to expect a wide range of problems, including a very low IQ and inability to read or drive a car. I was told by a physical therapist that Presley was "the lowest of low tone." Again and again, our family and friends told us, "We're so sorry." At one point, my husband suggested we consider giving our daughter up for adoption.

Through it all, I began to feel a sense of peace. I respected everyone's opinion, but I already knew Presley could do anything she wanted to do, and that no one could predict her future cognitive and physical abilities. I knew God was giving me this peace and guidance.

By the time Presley was six months old, I felt we were going the way God wanted us to go. She was thriving, she was strong, and she was full of energy and personality. She was nothing like the flaccid, calm baby I had been warned to expect. I thought back to those initial confusing days and the tornado of emotions, and I knew I needed to write down everything I'd learned to inform new parents. I didn't want anyone else to experience the same negative, "lost" response that I had.

God spoke to me repeatedly for several weeks to begin putting this information together. Several people told me it was a waste of time. They assured me that there must be something already like it. I should just focus on the girls. Instead, I obeyed God. I stayed up late after everyone had gone to bed putting together a book of everything I needed after Presley was born. I wanted to compile something that was positive and gave detailed guidance. Finally, it was finished.

As part of my research, a friend and I went to the hospitals and clinics to meet with staff. We have become part of the Down Syndrome Association to get this book into the hands of new parents. The book has since been adopted by the Arkansas Down Syndrome Association, and we now receive calls from most of the hospitals to come meet the new parents and bring them a copy of the book. We stay in touch with the parents and introduce them to someone with a child close to their child's age and hometown. We bring a gourmet meal for a parents' night when the child returns to the hospital in about three months for heart surgery. We have also been able to sponsor four children for a special neurodevelopmental program.

The rewards have been more than I could have imagined. This was one time in my life that I listened to God and was immediately obedient.

Robin

LOVE'S PRICE

The blessings of God, however, may not be realized in this life. We have such a narrow focus—we want God's blessings right here, right now—but God isn't limited by time and space. We have the promise of blessings for obedience, but we often pay a price. Throughout history, Christians have suffered for their faith—and they've also suffered just for being born in a fallen world. We have the promise that someday in the new heaven and new earth, God will make all things right. Then and there, we will have resurrected and glorified bodies, no more sin, and the most fulfilling work we could imagine. Teresa of Ávila once remarked, "In light of heaven, the worst suffering on earth will be seen to be no more serious than one night in an inconvenient hotel."[10]

People are happy that Christ paid a price, but they don't like the idea that loving and obeying God requires a price from us. I did a sermon series on suffering a year or two ago. By the second week, our online audience was half what it had been at the beginning. When the series was over, most of them came back. The message was clear: tell us what we want to hear, but leave out the challenging parts of the Christian message. I'm sorry, but I can't do that. God calls us to be disciples, followers of Christ. When we follow His example, we notice His character, His courage, and His willingness to suffer to accomplish the Father's will. For Jesus, paying the price wasn't a surprise. That's why He came! We need to get a better grip on what a robust faith in Jesus means for today.

In his book, *Crazy Love,* Francis Chan observed, "People who are *obsessed* with Jesus aren't consumed with their personal safety and comfort above all else. Obsessed people care more about God's kingdom coming to this earth than their own lives being shielded from pain or distress."[11]

The church has grown stronger and bigger during times of persecution, famine, and plague. I'm not suggesting that we need to pray for those things, but we should at least be wise enough to recognize that calamities (on any scale from personal to global) give Christians an opportunity to be humble, sacrificial, and compassionate to those around them. When we choose kindness instead of revenge, and live generously instead of selfishly, we shine in the darkness like beacons on a hill.

The sacrifice we make may be monetary, or we may sacrifice time and attention. Mothers of young children know what it means to give themselves to clean spit up off the floor and clothes, wash endless loads of laundry, wipe crying eyes, and prepare meals that may or may not be eaten.

Billy Simpson discovered God's blessing through sacrifice. He wrote this letter:

> *Good morning, Pastor Rod!*
>
> *A friend of mine has owed me a sizable amount of money for almost a year for services I provided. I decided to write him a letter, but instead of trying to collect the money, I cancelled the debt completely! I told him, "Normally, I would never do such a thing. I don't work for free, but I felt impressed to pay this issue forward."*
>
> *You must understand how difficult this was for me. I'm still unemployed and have been for nineteen months. I really could have used the cash!*

As soon as I had composed the letter, I experienced a great sense of absolute peace—the same peace you mentioned in your message on obedience last night. Obedience to God is always rewarded.

Billy

CONSIDER THIS . . .

1. What are some ways people can be enslaved to behaviors, substances, and other people? What are the effects of this slavery on their time, attention, finances, and relationships?

2. Why is it important to realize immediate obedience is on a learning curve? What happens when a person assumes it will be easy, quick, and complete?

3. Since you began reading this book, have you become more aware
    of God's voice speaking to you through the Scriptures and in other
    ways? If so, how have you responded?

4. What would happen to you if God blessed your disobedience?

5. Explain the statement: The best and safest place is in the center of God's will.

6. If the proof of our love is obedience, and Jesus' sacrifice is the ultimate form of love, why do so many western Christians assume loving God won't involve any form of sacrifice and suffering? What happens to our faith when we have this view?

7. On a scale of 0 (zip) to 10 (completely), rate yourself on how your obedience to God reveals your love for Him. Explain your answer.

8. When was a time in your life when your love for God was rich and real? Ask God to reveal Himself again so that your love is renewed.

5

CONNECTION FAILURE

"We both believe, and disbelieve a hundred times an hour,
which keeps believing nimble."
—Emily Dickinson

O kay, let's be honest. Sometimes we don't hear God very clearly . . . and sometimes we don't want to hear Him at all. We don't have unfettered communication with the Lord. Unlike Adam and Eve walking with God in the garden before sin rocked their world (and ours), we encounter a variety of obstacles that impede first our ability to hear, and then our willingness to obey. But amazingly, even when fear and doubt cloud our hearts, God keeps whispering to us.

My son Tyler is a whiz at chemistry and an excellent student, so he enrolled in pre-pharmacy at the University of Arkansas-Little Rock. No one doubted he would do well in school and excel in his chosen profession. He had green lights all the way.

After a successful first year, God changed the trajectory of Tyler's life. He clearly sensed the Lord telling him to go into the ministry. He was excited about serving the Lord in that way, but he was worried how Cindy and I would respond. (Really? Are you kidding? How in the world would he think we wouldn't approve?) He had a full scholarship at UALR, and he knew the change of direction would be costly. He really thought the news would upset us, so he didn't say a word for weeks.

One Sunday morning, Tyler was really conflicted. His fears were as real as God's calling, and he didn't know what to do. He walked into our church welcome center where he was approached by Wilma DeFoggi, a long-time member. Like Anna, the woman who spoke to Joseph and Mary when they first took Jesus to the temple, Wilma is an older, wise, and perceptive person. She looked deep into his eyes, and said, "Tyler, I have a word from God for you."

My son was a bit surprised, but not shocked. He knew that God often speaks prophetically through others. He swallowed hard and nodded.

Wilma told him, "The Lord has a higher calling on your life." She paused for a second, and then announced, "God has been speaking to you, and you need to obey Him. Stop worrying. You can trust that He will work everything out. Don't be afraid. He knows what's best for you."

With renewed courage, Tyler told Cindy and me what God had put on his heart, and how worried he had been that the change would cost us so much money. We assured him that we were thrilled, and that God would provide. After putting off telling us for so long, he felt greatly relieved.

Tyler enrolled in Southwestern Assemblies of God University. Two months later I was asked to join the board of the school. After I accepted the position, I discovered that my children, specifically Tyler, would receive a scholarship for his tuition.

Tyler's experience demonstrates that several factors can be obstacles to obedience. There are, I'm afraid, more than we can count! Let's look at a few of them.

GOD'S INSTRUCTIONS MAKE NO SENSE

Quite often, we respond to God's whispers by saying, "What? You've got to be kidding." We have to remember that God is omniscient—He sees the beginning and the end, and He knows how every detail will fit together in His grand plan. Mountain climbers understand that sometimes to make progress up a cliff, they first have to go downward to access a better path. Before they begin, they carefully map out their route so there are no surprises. However, God seldom provides us with detailed maps. We have to trust that He knows exactly what direction we need to go and that He will provide clear instructions as they are needed. Sometimes when we're trying to climb He sends us in a direction that appears to be backwards, or to the base of a cliff, or into a cave. Only with confidence in our wise and loving King will we respond in faith when we don't understand His directives.

In the pages of Scripture, we see what can happen when men and women respond to God's strange directions:

- Moses led his people to the edge of a sea where they were defenseless against Pharaoh's army, but God miraculously opened the sea to let them escape.

- God reduced Gideon's army from 32,000 to 300 before a decisive battle.

- David fought a giant with only a slingshot.

- Meshach, Shadrach, and Abednego trusted God as they were thrown into a flaming furnace.

- Joseph believed Mary was honest when she told him the Holy Spirit had made her pregnant.

- Jesus knew the only hope for mankind was a seemingly tragic and senseless death.

God sometimes leads us to do things that are difficult to understand—for us and for those who are watching us.

The reverse, however, isn't necessarily true. If an impression makes no sense, we shouldn't assume it is God speaking. Sometimes we're just dumb. We hear things that God hasn't said, and we do things that He hasn't told us to do.

Still, it seems clear that God sometimes leads us to do things that are difficult to understand—for us and for those who are watching us. Many commands fly in the face of our culture and human nature.

- We give away at least ten percent of our income, even when our finances are tight.

- We make sure others receive honor instead of jockeying for attention and applause.

- We forgive those who have betrayed us, lied to us, and intentionally made our lives miserable.

- We reach out to help people who can never pay us back.

- We turn the other cheek when someone wrongs us.

- We leave a comfortable home and lucrative job to serve in poverty and obscurity.

If we believe God's instructions must fit our preconceived ideas of what He wants us to be and do, there will be no adventure in following Him. And we won't grow because we won't have to trust Him. When everything makes perfect sense, we can say, "Man, I made a great decision!" But when we follow God to places that are uncomfortable, we have to say, "Wow, I was scared, but God did miraculous things. He gets all the glory!"

The Bible doesn't say, "Without reason, it's impossible to please God." It says that without *faith* it is impossible to please Him (Heb. 11:6).

Patrick got a taste of the excitement of being available to God. By his own admission, he has lived his life "in his head." There's nothing wrong with being thoughtful and reflective, but Patrick is beginning to add the adventure of responding in faith when he hears God's voice. He sent me this letter:

Pastor Rod,

I've been a Christian for many years, but there's something about your messages on immediate obedience that is really attractive . . . and really threatening to me. I've always wanted God to explain the reasons behind His commands, but now I realize faith means I won't always know the reason why—I'll probably seldom know. After I heard your messages, I told the Lord that I wasn't sure how this works, but I was willing to give it a shot.

A couple of hours later, I was in a doctor's waiting room. It looked like everyone had been there a long time, and I wasn't thrilled about wasting several hours—especially around sick people. I chose one of the hundreds of old magazines from the table and prepared for a long wait. A young man was sitting next to me. He looked bored to death. Then I remembered the principle, and I prayed, "Lord, I have no idea if this will go anywhere, but I'm available to talk to this guy if You want me to. I'm listening."

For a long time, both of us just sat there. I assumed this wasn't a "God moment." Then suddenly he turned to me and asked a question. I don't even remember what it was, but in a few minutes we were talking about the Lord. He was new to the area and wanted to find a good church for himself, his wife, and their son.

He lives in a different part of town many miles from my home (and the doctor's office), but I told him about a great church near where he lives. When the nurse called his name and he walked back to see the doctor, he turned and thanked me for helping him. I replied, "It's my pleasure."

I sure hope I remember to ask God to make me sensitive to His voice. It's pretty cool when God turns nothing into something eternally significant!

Patrick

DISAPPROVAL

Ironically, God's people can be our most vocal opponents when we try to hear God's voice and obey Him. They claim they're looking out for our best interests (and they may be sincere in this), but our faith may threaten them, and it may cost them.

I have a friend who believes God is leading him to be a missionary in a Muslim country. He's read about Christians being persecuted and murdered—and many friends and family members have read the same accounts. They ask, "Will you and your family be safe? How can you guarantee nothing will happen to you and them?" He has no guarantee of safety. He accepts this fact; they don't.

People won't always stand and cheer for us when we obey God. Parents, grandparents, and friends don't like it when we move kids and grandkids across the country or around the world in answer to God's summons. Other people aren't threatened; they just think we're nuts. Radical obedience and glad sacrifice simply make no sense to them. However, those who have learned to practice listening and obeying are far more likely to affirm us as we pursue God with all our hearts.

Virtually all the heroes in the Bible faced fierce opposition from people who had a lot to lose from the person's faithfulness. We celebrate their faith because we see "the rest of the story." We know how God used them to rescue individuals and nations, but those people first had to muster the courage to act in the face of criticism and hostility.

Sometimes people tell me what they think I should be, say, or do. My usual response is, "Thanks. I'll pray about it." Some people get really upset when I don't jump to obey them. My calling is to obey

God, not people. If people's approval is our goal, we'll become chameleons, changing our color to suit the person and the moment. Paul faced the same pressure. He defiantly told the Galatians that he had a clear choice: "Am I now trying to win the approval of human beings, or of God? Or am I trying to please people? If I were still trying to please people, I would not be a servant of Christ" (Gal. 1:10).

Whenever we choose to obey God, we can expect honest questions, resistance, and occasional ridicule. Most of the time the negative reaction of those around us isn't some grand, orchestrated plot to stop us. It's just human nature. If they cheer our faithfulness, they have to be willing to be sensitive and responsive to God, too, and that makes them uncomfortable.

People who try to restrict our obedience by words of disapproval seldom come back later and admit, "Wow, I was so wrong. I appreciate your obedience to God even when people like me tried to stop you." That kind of honesty and repentance may happen occasionally, but not often.

Here's my promise: If you sign up to hear God's voice and respond obediently, you'll face disapproval and criticism. When it happens, don't be surprised. Keep listening, keep trusting, and keep obeying.

A COMPETITIVE SPIRIT

In *17 Irrefutable Laws of Teamwork*, John Maxwell outlines the benefits and liabilities of "The Law of the Scoreboard."[12] In companies and on teams, it's important to know what's important. A scoreboard gives important benchmarks for goals and progress, but it has a dark side.

Keeping score can bring out the worst in us, the drive to win at all costs, and even worse, the compulsion to be on top by putting others down.

Some people might think that being sensitive and responsive to the Spirit is a sure safeguard against the dark side of scorekeeping, but they're wrong. Sadly, the desire for oneupmanship is a built-in component in the human condition. Pastors, lay leaders, and faithful Christians aren't exempt. We just do it with a smile.

A few years ago, the Holy Spirit revealed a twisted motive for success in my life. To be honest, I was consumed with our church's growth. I tried to tell myself it was for God's glory, but the Spirit revealed that at least part of the motivation was self-validation. I wanted to look successful to other pastors.

Competition operates in a narrow sphere. Doctors aren't jealous of artists or lawyers. They're jealous of the applause other doctors receive. Lawyers envy lawyers, artists envy artists, and pastors envy pastors. In his classic work, *Mere Christianity*, C. S. Lewis observed:

"Pride gets no pleasure out of having something, only out of having more of it than the next man. We say that people are proud of being rich, or clever, or good-looking, but they are not. They are proud of being richer, or cleverer, or better-looking than others. If everyone else became equally rich, or clever, or good-looking there would be nothing to be proud about. It is the comparison that makes you proud; the pleasure of being above the rest. Once the element of competition is gone, pride has gone. That is why I say that Pride is essentially competitive in a way the other vices are not."[13]

A competitive spirit poisons our hearts. It can drive us to try to listen to God and obey Him—not to honor Him, but to prove we're more sensitive to God than anyone else! Then, we do right things for wrong reasons.

I spent an entire year praying against the spirit of competition in my heart. It was a year well spent. My competitive nature is not entirely gone, but it has been greatly reduced. At least now I'm not surprised when the Spirit shows me that it has raised its ugly head, and I know what to do about it. Now I can truly celebrate "kingdom wins" instead of "Rod wins." Obedience doesn't always lead to a visible, personal success story. If we're obeying for that reason, it will be all about us and not about Christ.

> I believe that God often—and maybe usually—asks us to sacrifice the external thing we value more than Him.

Recently our church staff discussed some important questions: "Is our church too big? Are we making genuine disciples of Jesus Christ? Or are we just putting on a big show?" It was a wonderful conversation. If our goal is only to be bigger than other churches, we will never ask those questions, and if we do, we'll find a way to justify a relentless pursuit of size.

I believe that God often—and maybe usually—asks us to sacrifice the external thing we value more than Him. God may require us to give up prestige, popularity, comfort, or position. For instance, if popularity is the scoreboard we live by, God will probably ask us to go out of our way to be a friend to someone who is awkward and alone.

When old Abraham put his affections too much on his son instead of the One who gave him a son, God asked Abraham to take Isaac up to the mountain and sacrifice him. On that occasion, God honored the old dad's faith and spared the son. In our case, He requires us to give up the thing that has captured our hearts. Sometimes He returns it to us; sometimes He doesn't. It's His call.

THE HABIT OF DISOBEDIENCE

For obedience to become instinctive, we have to retrain our minds and hearts to respond to God. Disobedience, though, doesn't require much training—we do it naturally! The promises of advertising, our envious nature, the example set by many families, and human nature all tell us that personal happiness is the ultimate goal and selfishness is the only reasonable lifestyle.

We expect pagans to be disobedient to God. They have no connection with Him and no desire to please Him. Sadly, many who call themselves Christians aren't much different from their unbelieving neighbors. They may attend church and be involved in some activities, but Christ exists in an isolated compartment of their lives. For them, He certainly isn't *Lord of all,* and to be honest, He's not even Lord *at* all.

A habitually disobedient person's heart becomes hardened to God and apathetic about His purposes. The wonder, joy, and adventure of following the King aren't even on the radar. The psalmist used the carrot of God's love and the stick of His wrath to warn people:

"Come, let us bow down in worship, let us kneel before the LORD our Maker; for he is our God and we are the people of his pasture, the flock under his care. Today, if only you would hear his voice, 'Do not harden your hearts as you did at Meribah, as you did that day at Massah in the wilderness, where your ancestors tested me; they tried me, though they had seen what I did. For forty years I was angry with that generation; I said, 'They are a people whose hearts go astray, and they have not known my ways.' So I declared on oath in my anger, 'They shall never enter my rest'" (Ps. 95:6–11).

We may laugh at people doing stupid things on sitcoms, but spiritual disobedience isn't a joke. It's an indication of a heart that has drifted away from devotion to the God who deserves our complete love and loyalty. And disobedience in one area is seldom isolated. When a person is disobedient and falling apart in a marriage, his finances are often a wreck, too . . . and his health, and his career, and his friendships, and so forth.

A wife came to see me about her husband's affair. As we talked, I asked, "Have you taken a good look at your family finances?"

She looked surprised and shook her head, "Why would I have any concerns about our money? He had an affair. He didn't steal anything."

I repeated, "It would be smart to look at your checkbook, your savings accounts, and any other investments and credit cards."

She thought I was being too reactionary, but three days later she called to tell me that her husband had taken more than $20,000 out of an investment account. "I have no idea where the money went," she sobbed.

Disobedience is like an iceberg: often a lot more is hidden than what we see on the surface. The first act of disobedience naturally leads to more and increasingly severe disobedience. It's an ever-expanding cycle.

The Bible doesn't try to soften the point; it labels the habit of disobedience: *rebellion* against God. It's possible for people to become so hardened that God "gives them over" to their sinful desires (Rom. 1:24). God invites them to follow Him for a long time, but at some point He reluctantly lets them learn the hard way. He says, "If this is what you want, it's all yours. The sin you find delicious will ruin your life and those you love, but it's entirely your choice."

THE FEAR OF FAILURE AND EMBARRASSMENT

When discussing the challenge of becoming immediately obedient, many people have asked, "Pastor, what if I get it wrong? What if I think I hear God say something, but it isn't Him at all?"

I assure them that the standard of success isn't 100 percent, and I say, "Don't worry about it. Yes, you'll get it wrong sometimes. We all occasionally misunderstand the people we love. It happens in marriage and with our closest friends. God is far more inscrutable than a husband or a wife, so you can be sure you will fail to understand His voice from time to time." Like the parents of a little child, God delights when we try, and when we get up after we've failed. I often tell people, "I'd rather try to do good in God's name and be a little off than do nothing out of fear and miss what God had for me."

But the issue most people are worried about isn't failure; it's that other people notice they have failed. They aren't too worried about mis-understanding, but they're terrified of catching grief from others who might laugh at them for being so stupid as to think that God would really speak to them!

The fear of embarrassment also causes people to go through with decisions they know aren't God's best. I applaud men and women who have the guts to call off a wedding, refuse a promotion, or walk away from an opportunity because God shows them it's not His will.

LAZINESS

"Discipline" isn't a dirty word. To learn to do anything well, we must devote time and energy to understand the processes and develop the skills. It's interesting that many people see spiritual life in a completely different sphere from other pursuits in their lives. They think nothing of investing money and time in learning the techniques of fly-fishing, growing roses, playing golf, or mastering a computer program. But they assume developing a rich, dynamic relationship with God should come effortlessly. It doesn't.

A flywheel is a good metaphor for the effort required to make a habit out of immediate obedience. Inertia is a reality. It takes a lot of energy to start the wheel turning. (At first, it seems to require far too much effort!) Soon, the same amount of effort makes the wheel turn faster . . . and faster . . . and faster.

In the same way, we must overcome inertia in our spiritual lives. The first "pushes" of immediate obedience require a lot of effort, partly because we haven't used those muscles very much. After a while, each push is more efficient, and we see more results.

Obedience is *hard at the beginning*, but it becomes easier and more rewarding as the habit is formed. Disobedience is *easy at the beginning*, but it becomes more difficult and complicated as the consequences bog us down. Choose obedience.

PICKING THE WRONG FRIENDS

Faith-filled friends celebrate obedience and create a healthy atmosphere, but the last thing disobedient friends want is for you to follow God. The more you obey and see God work, the more their disobedience becomes evident. They put pressure on you to revert to their disbelieving mold. In many cases they remain your friend only if you give up your commitment to follow hard after God's heart.

I've known a lot of people who made dramatic decisions to trust God by walking out of a life of addiction or promiscuity and walking into a life of adventure by obeying Him, only to have their "friends" pull them back.

Our choice of friends matters. It *really* matters. For many people, the negative impact of friends is the most powerful obstacle that prevents them from following Christ. The proverb says it succinctly and accurately, "Walk with the wise and become wise, for a companion of fools suffers harm" (Prov. 13:20).

When I talk to people who have been dragged down by a network of caustic, unbelieving friends, I ask them to do two things: find some new friends, and change their cellphone number. If they're unwilling to look for people who will be a positive influence (maybe a small group, maybe a pastor or a counselor, or maybe a rehab clinic), the power of their current friendships will almost certainly block their progress. And if they're not willing to change their phone number, I know they're still emotionally hooked into the people of their past. Connection and access make all the difference. If they make those changes, a world of hope and opportunity opens in front of them.

NO VISION FOR CHANGE

Few of us change because we read a book. Books fill our minds with concepts and inspire us with stories, but life change happens most readily when we see a model of the goal we're shooting for, and we have people around us who are cheering us on.

I'm so thankful for my parents. They modeled a sensitive heart, ears that were listening to God, and a commitment to obey Him instantly. Day after day, I saw them pursue God and respond to Him in faith. Occasionally, their obedience cost them; far more often, it was a delight. No matter what happened, I was sure they were radically committed to follow God wherever He led them.

My parents budgeted money every month to use however God led them to use it. It was "God's slush fund." When God told them to give money to a poor person, a struggling neighbor, or a missionary, they were ready. Because I saw it modeled, the joy of giving—and the preparation for it—has been a regular part of my life. I treasure the memories of my parents' generosity, and I hope my boys are storing up the same kinds of memories.

Modeling a tender heart and a rigorous commitment to obey God is one of the best gifts we can give our kids. This kind of example doesn't just happen. It must be intentional. We have to build it into our schedules and priorities.

Of course, many people grew up in families where loving and following God weren't priorities or passions! Abuse and abandonment crush the souls of many, but their fate isn't hopeless. God has given us another family—His family. In authentic and honest connections with the family of God, we can watch other believers as they make choices to listen to God and respond to Him in faith. As we watch them, we follow their example and we learn the lessons we missed when we were kids.

> Modeling a tender heart and a rigorous commitment to obey God is one of the best gifts we can give our kids.

The New Testament letters presume believers are in strong relationships with one another. Most of the churches were small, and Christians were often persecuted, so it's not surprising they valued the love and support they received from each other. We have to work hard to make sure we attend to the training of people who are genuine disciples. The Bible says that as leaders model a lifestyle of immediate obedience, the rest of the people watch and learn.

In Paul's letter to the Ephesians, he described the impact of leaders:

"So Christ himself gave the apostles, the prophets, the evange-
lists, the pastors and teachers, to equip his people for works of
service, so that the body of Christ may be built up until we all
reach unity in the faith and in the knowledge of the Son of God
and become mature, attaining to the whole measure of the full-
ness of Christ. Then we will no longer be infants, tossed back
and forth by the waves, and blown here and there by every
wind of teaching and by the cunning and craftiness of people
in their deceitful scheming. Instead, speaking the truth in love,
we will grow to become in every respect the mature body of
him who is the head, that is, Christ" (Eph. 4:11–15).

If you're in relationships where you can see other people model
a sensitive and responsive heart, treasure them. If you aren't spending
time with people like that, find them. It's essential.

ABSENCE OF SPIRITUAL AUTHORITY

Is it the chicken or the egg? Are people disobedient because they
lack spiritual authority, or do they lack spiritual authority because
they're disobedient? Either way, these people don't benefit from the
God-appointed leadership that can inspire and direct them. Some
people insist their spiritual lives are "private." They say, "I'm a Christian,
and I believe in God, but I don't want to be part of any church." They
often see the pastor as their enemy—or at least as a nuisance.

People with no respect for spiritual authority seldom (if ever) have a sensitive and responsive heart of obedience to God. Respect for one feeds respect for the other. If you can't have a healthy response to the human authorities God has put over you, it's unlikely you'll be able to trust and obey the mysterious, infinite, invisible God.

ABUSIVE AUTHORITY

Spiritual authorities in the church are thoroughly human. They often do magnificent things, but sometimes they fail miserably and hurt the flock God has entrusted to them. They may have used "God told me" to intimidate and control their people. Spiritual abuse is one of the most tragic things I've ever seen, and it doesn't heal easily. I have talked to individuals who were spiritually manipulated by a pastor decades ago and are still reluctant to trust anyone in authority over them. This grieves me deeply. Quite often, those people transfer their suspicion and bitterness to all spiritual authorities—including me. They resist my offer to help them heal the gaping wounds from the past, and they stay stuck in their wounds and cynicism.

Spiritual authorities have a high standard to keep. God has commanded leaders of the church to be diligent shepherds. Peter commanded, "Be shepherds of God's flock that is under your care, watching over them—not because you must, but because you are willing, as God wants you to be; not pursuing dishonest gain, but eager to serve; not lording it over those entrusted to you, but being examples to the flock. And when the Chief Shepherd appears, you will receive the crown of glory that will never fade away" (1 Peter 5:2–4). Good spiritual leaders are to be actively involved in getting to know people's hopes and needs, and in caring for them in specific ways. Their leadership should be marked by sacrifice, compassion, and love. As they lead, they are to follow the example of Christ, and they have the promise of reward for their faithful, loving service.

It's not just *spiritual* authority that's a major obstacle to a life of obedience to God. People who have been abused or abandoned by their parents or any other adult often transfer their pain and defenses to protect themselves from all other authorities, including God and church leaders. Those deeply hurt individuals may go through the motions of church, but until the past wounds are healed, they won't trust God or people. Those who had distant or abusive parents struggle to trust their heavenly Father.

FEAR OF CONSEQUENCES

We pay a price for our obedience; the cost can be real or imaginary. When God tells us to give $100 to someone, we know the price tag. When He directs us to visit an elderly person who has no family, we know it will cost us some time out of our schedule. When God whispers to take a colleague to lunch to share the gospel, we know it will cost a little money. But those aren't our real worries. We're much more afraid of the unknown. What will happen to our reputation when people realize we're sold out to God? Will God tell us to do something bizarre? Will He ruin our lives?

Yes, there's always a cost for obedience, but we have the promise that God will reward us—here, hereafter, or both—if we respond to

Him in faith. We can offer a million excuses, but none of them carry any weight in light of God's surpassing wisdom to guide us, power to change lives, and unlimited resources to provide what we need to do His will. God doesn't begin His instructions with "When you have time," or "If it's convenient," or "If you can spare

Yes, there's always a cost for obedience, but we have the promise that God will reward us—here, hereafter, or both— if we respond to Him in faith.

some money." When He directs, He either has already provided or we can be sure He will provide. Our task is to act in faith—and to act immediately.

God may give us directions to see how far we are willing to trust Him. Years ago, God put Detroit on my heart. As I prayed, the city kept coming back to my mind. It seemed Detroit was in the news every night and in the paper every morning. I'm pretty slow, but I realized God was trying to tell me something: I needed to be willing to move my family to Detroit and have a ministry there.

For several months, I didn't tell anybody about this impression. I read everything I could find about the city of Detroit and studied detailed maps of the city and the surrounding suburbs. Finally, I called Alton Garrison, a friend I trust, and explained that I was confused. I said, "God has put Detroit on my heart, but I don't know what to do about it. I don't know if I'm supposed to plant a satellite church there, or if I'm supposed to move there with my family and start a church. All I know is that God won't let me get this city off my mind."

Alton made a connection for me with some church leaders in Michigan. That was the trigger. At that point, we held a family meeting where I told Cindy and the boys what God had put on my heart. I told them I wasn't sure what it all meant, but I wanted us to pray and plan together. I asked them to be open to the Lord.

They responded with surprise and support. Tyler is a big Dallas Mavericks fan. I knew it would be hard for him to leave his favorite team, but he immediately said, "Dad, I can learn to cheer for the Pistons."

Parker said, "I love it here, but if this is what God has for us, I'll do it."

Cindy told me, "Let's see what God has for us in Detroit. We'll be obedient to whatever He tells us to do."

Our family commitment is to be spiritually ready. We want to live in a way that we can walk away from everything in sixty days. If we can't, there are too many barricades between the Lord and us. I felt sure that was precisely what God was calling us to do.

The next Monday morning, I flew to Detroit. I sat with my earbuds in, listening to worship music, praying, and crying my eyes out. I didn't want to leave our church in North Little Rock, but I was going to follow the Lord wherever He might lead me. It was a confusing and challenging time.

Unexpectedly, I felt a tap on my shoulder. I opened my eyes and saw a lady leaning over me. She handed me a wad of money and said above the roar of the engines, "I don't know what this is about, but God told me to give this to you. He told me to tell you that He knows exactly what's going on with you." She returned to her seat.

I spent a day and a half in Detroit, but nothing clicked. I didn't find a partner, I didn't sense God's confirmation . . . nothing. I flew back home, as confused as ever.

A few days later, I realized that the whole emphasis on Detroit wasn't about the city or moving my family. God was testing me to see how far I was willing to go to obey Him. A move to Detroit would have shaken my family's world, but we were all willing to go. It was a test for me, for Cindy, and for Parker and Tyler. For some reason, God wanted us all to put our comfortable, exciting, familiar lives in North Little Rock on the altar and be willing to give it all to Him. It was like He was saying, "Rod, it's easy to *say* you will obey Me, but are you willing to walk away from everything and truly follow Me? 'Foxes have holes and birds have nests, but the Son of Man has nowhere to lay His head.' Are you willing to uproot your family? What if obedience costs you . . . and costs you a lot?"

The confusing months helped me listen to the voice of God, count the cost, suffer the consequences, and obey Him. And the lady on the plane? To this day, I have no idea what that was about. I gave the money to the missions offering the next Sunday. I think God may have been using her to cheer me on: "Good job, Rod! You've been listening, and you're on the plane. This lady is your own personal pep squad. You're exactly where you're supposed to be: confused but trusting. Way to go!"

BENCHMARK

I carefully avoid telling people how and when God will speak to them. God is mysterious and majestic. The King can do whatever He wants to do. He can speak in any way and as often as He chooses. The question we need to be most concerned about is whether we are listening and responding.

Even though I avoid any guarantees—or any kind of predictable expectations—of God's voice, I think it's wise to regularly consider a different perspective. If you're *not* hearing anything, something's probably wrong. If you go a month without being prompted to give something to a person, or if you go that long without sensing an impression to go out of our way to show kindness, you need to ask:

- "Am I really listening to God?"

- "Do I sense His presence and love when I pray, or am I just going through the motions?"

- "Did I hear Him, but not obey?"

- "Do I need to go back to the last thing God told me to do and obey Him in that matter before I expect to hear something new?"

Occasionally God takes us through a prolonged time of darkness, but such instances are rare and need to be confirmed by a wise, mature person who knows us well. Otherwise, we should expect to hear from Him—at least once in a while. If we don't, we've experienced a connection failure.

IT'S WORTH IT

You can always find reasons to avoid obeying God, but if you find the courage to respond to Him with a faithful heart, you can be sure it's worth it. You will receive far more than you give—not always in tangible ways, but rather in knowing that God is using you to advance His kingdom . . . and even more, that He is pleased with you.

Mike Winslow gave up something he valued and found it was worth the price.

> *Pastor Rod,*
>
> *Last Wednesday night during worship, I distinctly sensed God calling me to obey Him in a specific way. I wrestled with Him over it. "Was that really God? Or was that just my compassionate inclination? I can't give all of it! Are you sure?"*
>
> *The next couple days I was annoyed, I tried to rationalize, and I was sad because I was not immediately eager to obey fully. But I got over it. Really, what did I have to lose? I had plans. I had some things I wanted. But obeying God is the proof of allegiance. If my heart truly belongs to Him, why not obey?*
>
> *So I did. This afternoon I delivered about $3,500 of drum equipment to a tenth grader who was in desperate need of tools to hone his craft of worshiping our Savior on the drums.*
>
> *As I look back on my notes from your lessons on obedience, two reasons why we must obey jump off the page at me:*
>
> *"The practice of immediate obedience lets me experience God's perfect timing." This student needed tools now!*

"Immediate obedience is not about me being the hero. It's about God getting the glory." I'm so grateful for a heavenly Father who has patience with me even when my initial reaction is selfish. No doubt God will be glorified with Josh's drumming.

Pastor Rod, I love you. Again, thanks for challenging me.

God must increase—I must decrease,

Mike

And Edward sensed God leading him to give—when it made no sense.

Pastor Rod,

I just wanted to let you know something that happened to me, and all due to obeying God. I'm in the middle of moving my business. Of course, moving is always expensive, and the new landlord threw in some unexpected costs. Quite frankly, I didn't have it in my budget, but I was too far into it and too close to the move schedule to back out. I'd been praying that God would take care of it, and as long as I was obeying Him, I knew He would, though I didn't know how.

On Sunday morning after hearing the story of the mission effort in Benin, I felt I should give from my business to that cause, even though I knew it was definitely not helping my budget. Of course, I did the back and forth: Was that really God wanting me to do that, or was it just me? I figured, hey, either way, it's helping God's kingdom.

I was still asking God for help on the finances and wasn't sure what would happen. I got a text from the landlord this morning saying they were not going to charge me rent in the month of February, and I would just pick up with the rent in March on the new place. It was out of the blue. I hadn't said anything to them about working with me on it.

This will make it possible for me to be within my planned budget and also do what I need to do to make the move happen with a lot less stress. As a bonus, I looked in my bank account and found an influx of extra cash into the business at just the right time.

I always think back to your statement that there is no such thing as coincidence when God is involved. This is just another example.

I thought you'd like to hear another story of how obedience really pays off—literally, in this instance!

Edward

So, no more excuses and no more delays. Be honest about any negative thoughts and resistant feelings. Focus your attention on God's greatness and grace, and take the step God is telling you to take.

CONSIDER THIS . . .

1. When you get an instruction from God that doesn't make sense, what characteristics of God remind you that you can trust Him even when you don't understand? How would this reflection on His character change your perspective and your actions?

2. For you, which is more of an obstacle: the fear of failure or the fear of embarrassment? Explain your answer.

3. Do you think men or women struggle more with a competitive spirit? Explain your answer.

4. Has there been a time in your life when friends influenced you in a negative way? How do you wish you had responded?

5. Who is in your life now that encourages you, speaks truth to you, and helps you walk with God?

6. Do you have an innate trust or distrust of authority? Where do you think this perspective came from?

7. Which of the obstacles in this chapter are the greatest threats to your commitment to obey God immediately? What resources can you use to overcome them?

6

THE PERILS OF DISOBEDIENCE

"As long as your sin breaks your heart, as long as your disobedience makes
you lie awake nights and wet your pillow in tears, there is hope for you.
But when you become contented with your wickedness, when you come to
believe that it is the best possible for you, then you are in danger indeed."
—Clovis G. Chappell

When you say no to God's whispers and nudges, at least two people lose: you, and the one God wanted to touch through you. Becca wrote me about how easy it was to turn away from God's leading.

> *Recently I went on a trip with my husband. He was going to run*
> *in a race, so I took a copy of* The Scarlet Letter *to read. I would soon*
> *be teaching it to juniors in high school, but I had not read it since I*
> *was that age, so it was pretty imperative that I get caught up.*
>
> *Waiting for the race to end, I was stretched out in the sun-*
> *shine and turning some serious pages in the book. Suddenly, a guy*
> *approached me and said, "You're an English teacher." I thought*
> *that was more than a lucky guess since probably nobody in their*
> *right mind would leisurely read nineteenth-century American*

literature at a sporting event, but I confirmed that yes, I was an English teacher. I resumed reading.

He didn't move. He then said, "At a high school in Arkansas." Now he had my attention. I looked him full in the face, and he smiled. I thought I recognized him, but I couldn't place him.

He didn't wait for me to ask who he was. "I'm Brent," he said.

I can count on one hand the number of kids in my classes I've ever had to write up. I want my administrators to know that when they get one of my kids in the office, something substantial has happened. Brent was one of those kids. He was a student during my first year as a teacher. He told me he had recognized me earlier that day at the race, but couldn't get to me. He was glad to run into me again.

Brent talked with me about his family. He explained that he was at the race watching his wife compete—but that she actually wasn't his wife, even though she "might as well be." He said they had a daughter together. He was really putting it all out there, and there were plenty of openings for me to ask questions. I felt a nudge to delve deeper into conversation, but I needed to finish The Scarlet Letter. I made polite, yet increasingly disinterested replies, the kind you make when bowing out of a conversation. I told him it was good to see him, and I resumed reading.

I didn't even realize I had missed it until the next day at a youth workers' meeting when someone was talking about a person God had placed in his path to minister to that week. When it hit me that I had missed my opportunity with Brent, I actually shouted,

"Oh, no!" I immediately prayed that God would either give me another opportunity with Brent, or that He would give Brent an opportunity to talk to a more responsive Christian who wouldn't be as thick-headed as I had been.

This incident happened months ago, but I still feel so guilty about it. How difficult would it have been for me to talk to Brent for just a few minutes? What would I have really lost? Some sleep later, finishing a book? Stupid!

Had I sustained it, the conversation may not have amounted to anything. I'll likely not know in this life. I do know that whatever Brent needed that day, God met through His provision. The part that grieves me is that I didn't get to be part of it. I missed it.

Becca

Disobedience never leads to good results. It never produces joy, confidence, and blessing. I've never heard anyone tell me:

"The best decision I ever made was disobeying God."

"I disobeyed God and kept my tithe to myself. It worked out great!"

"My marriage and kids were a mess, but I kept disobeying God by using anger to intimidate and control them. They really appreciate it! We're really close now."

"I knew God wanted me to stop and show kindness to a stranger, but I decided against it. I'm so glad I did."

"God instructed me to speak the hard but honest truth to a relative who's an addict, but I decided it would upset her, so I decided to stay quiet. She's still an addict, but I dodged a difficult conversation. It's wonderful!"

"God told me to give all I had in that offering. I thought about it, but no way. I'm really glad now I didn't listen to God. The extra stuff I was able to buy has given me true fulfillment."

"I knew it was wrong to date that girl, but I decided to do it my way instead of God's way. It was a great move! Our relationship is fantastic."

No, in all my years of observing people in various walks of life, I've concluded that the empirical evidence is crystal clear: sooner or later, disobedience always leads to heartache, alienation, and disaster.

Some people read the Scriptures or hear a message about obeying God's voice, and they complain, "I've tried to listen, but I don't hear anything from God. I guess it just doesn't work for me."

Wrong. Almost always, God has already told them to do something, but they haven't done it. They need to go back to their last point of disobedience, repent and obey, and then move forward with God.

Intentionally disobeying God is like putting earplugs in our spiritual ears. It makes it very hard to hear His voice the next time. And God is persistent. He keeps telling us to do the same thing until we respond in faith. As we've seen, He won't give us the *next* word until we've obeyed the *last* word.

Besides a guilty conscience and clogged ears, there are several other perils of refusing to obey God's voice.

DISOBEDIENCE LIMITS GOD'S BLESSINGS

You will never disobey yourself out of a problem. People come to me with all kinds of problems in their relationships and finances. I ask them what the Bible says they need to do. They usually know the biblical commands and principles that relate to their situations, but quite often, they insist they have a better way. I try not to laugh, but I often ask them, "Well, how has disobeying God worked for you so far?" Often, the lights come on at that moment, but others still don't understand what I'm trying to tell them.

> God delights in showering blessings on His children who actively and intentionally respond to His voice.

Parents reward obedient kids, but it would be foolish and irresponsible for them to give the same rewards to children who are passive or defiant. Rewarding them would only confirm them in their selfishness. In the same way, God delights in showering blessings on His children who actively and intentionally respond to His voice.

The story of the children of Israel is a graphic depiction of how God blesses obedience and withholds blessing for disobedience. When His people obeyed, God gave them a land flowing with milk and honey, a stable government, good harvests, and a fabulous temple in which to worship Him. When they chose to defy Him and worship idols, they suffered military defeats, terrible kings, famine, and cruel captivity in exile. After they came to their senses and realized how their disobedience had ruined their lives, they repented and returned to God . . . until they became complacent or defiant, and the cycle began again.

Most of the time, we can identify a clear cause and effect between obedience and blessing, and between disobedience and heartache. The prophet Samuel announced the consequences of King Saul's disobedience:

> "'The LORD has done what he predicted through me. The LORD has torn the kingdom out of your hands and given it to one of your neighbors—to David. Because you did not obey the LORD or carry out his fierce wrath against the Amalekites, the LORD has done this to you today. The LORD will deliver both Israel and you into the hands of the Philistines, and tomorrow you and your sons will be with me. The LORD will also give the army of Israel into the hands of the Philistines.' Immediately Saul fell full length on the ground, filled with fear because of Samuel's words" (1 Sam. 28:17–20).

I've talked to people who resented the fact that God blessed their friends who gave generously and sacrificially. They wonder why God hasn't blessed them. They haven't made the obvious connection between obedience and blessing.

People may look at the lives of Job, Jacob, Jesus and others in the Bible and conclude, "Well, obedience didn't work out very well for them!" But they need a bigger picture of God's purposes and His timing.

Each of those examples (and many others listed in Hebrews 11) suffered because they obeyed, but eventually, God honored them far more than they suffered. We can be completely confident in God's promise of blessing when we obey, but we need to be careful to avoid forcing Him into our timetable. We can get so focused on the route and schedule that we miss the destination.

In *Reaching for the Invisible God*, Philip Yancey noted that God's path for the patriarchs—Abraham, Isaac, and Jacob—was quite "puzzling." God's promises were often followed by infertility, delays, and disappointments. Yancey observes:

> "This tortuous path toward populating a great nation shows that God operates on a different timetable than impatient human beings expect. From Abraham, Isaac, and Jacob—and also Joseph, Moses, David, and a host of others—I learned that God moves in ways I would neither predict nor desire. Yet each of those Old Testament characters lived and died in faith, vowing to the end that God had indeed kept his promises."[14]

DISOBEDIENCE SPREADS LIKE A VIRUS

I've never known anyone who was disobedient in only one area of life. Disbelief may have started at a single point, but it invariably spreads to infect other areas. When a person ignores God about money, she doesn't listen to God about food or honesty or gossip or sleep or other parts of life.

God doesn't demand perfect obedience. Only one person has ever met that standard. But if we have any clue about the immensity of God's love and power, we will want His will more than anything else. When we close our ears and our hearts to Him because something seems hard or unreasonable, the result is an infection. If we recognize it and repent, the disease of doubt stops. But if we refuse to be honest with God about our faithlessness, it becomes easier to walk away from Him when we have the opportunity to disobey.

We often fear obedience, but we should be more afraid of the consequences of refusing to obey God. Saying no to Him results in the removal of His hand of protection and blessing; it delays His direction and quiets His voice . . . until we wake up and choose to obey.

> We often fear obedience, but we should be more afraid of the consequences of refusing to obey God.

If a virus takes over the body, organs fail and the person dies. If the disease of disbelief and disobedience takes over, the person's heart becomes hardened—lifeless, dull, and unresponsive. If a person is sick but refuses a medicine that can certainly cure him, we assume he has lost his mind. It's the same in the spiritual world. When we refuse the antidote of repentance and the cleansing of forgiveness, the disease of disobedience continues to spread and ruin our lives. When we let that happen, it's not amusing or clever; it only exposes our foolishness.

DISOBEDIENCE RESULTS IN REGRETS

I sometimes hear people say, "My goal in life is to be able to say before I die that I have no regrets." I applaud that sense of purpose, but it can only be achieved through a lifelong pursuit of God's voice, God's will, and God's paths. From my observations of people, I can categorically conclude that every regret is the direct result of a moment (or a pattern) of disobedience.

As I have listened to stories, I've heard numerous regrets from people:

- "I knew I shouldn't have married him."

- "I knew better than to drive after I'd been drinking."

- "I knew it was wrong, but . . ."

- "I lost my job—and my reputation—because I stole from my employer. What was I thinking?"

- "I felt a check in my spirit, but I ignored it and went ahead anyway. The result was a disaster."

In the saga of every broken heart, we find a moment when the person had a choice: to obey God or walk away from Him. In each of those tragic dramas, they chose disobedience.

It's not just "those people" who have made dumb mistakes and paid the price. When I look at my own life, I can easily point to moments when I had a clear opportunity to make a choice, and I chose disobedience. I each case, I wish I had made a different decision.

When God gives you an instruction, your obedience may provide short-term relief for the person God leads you to help . . . or it may make a much bigger impact. On some occasions, obeying God's directions are a matter of life and death. LaVonna wrote about her deepest regret:

> *Pastor Rod,*
>
> *When I was twenty-one years old, I was engaged to a future missionary and working to help my parents pay for our simple wedding. Starting at 2:00 a.m., I had the glamorous job of baking biscuits and frying chicken for a fast food restaurant. One Saturday morning an unexpected order for 500 pieces of chicken had everyone scrambling to keep up. I was up to my elbows in flour when my manager came back and introduced eighteen-year-old Richard to me. It was his first day to work, and he was to assist me with the order. I immediately objected, but my boss told me to continue making biscuits. He told Richard how to fry the chicken. I was frustrated, but had no choice but to comply. Richard had obviously never cooked anything in his short life and was all thumbs.*
>
> *While trying to keep calm and work at a frantic pace, I felt the Holy Spirit whisper, "Tell him about Me."*
>
> *I literally said out loud, "You have got to be kidding!"*
>
> *Richard's eyes were a bit unfocused, and he could barely string two sentences together. I guessed he had been smoking weed, or perhaps was hooked on drugs and alcohol. I sincerely doubted he would care to hear about God's love, and I suspected he would make fun of me if I broached the subject of his eternal destiny. I was intimidated to share my faith with someone "like him," and frankly, I just didn't have the time.*

Twice more, I heard the still, small voice, "Tell him about Me." After the third time, I muttered under my breath, "Okay, God. If the two of us have a break together, I'll tell him about You." Our breaks didn't coincide, so I concluded I was off the hook.

I left work exhausted that Saturday afternoon. The next day I enjoyed worshiping with my local body of believers. On Monday I came back to work refreshed because I didn't have to be there until 6:00 a.m.—the extra four hours of sleep was wonderful!

About halfway through my shift, I was again elbow deep in flour when another manager came by. She asked if I had heard what happened to Richard. She said that on Saturday evening after his shift, Richard met a group of friends. They were drinking and running around in a pickup truck. Several of them were riding in the bed. The driver lost control of the vehicle and hit a tree. Six of the eight in the truck were killed instantly, Richard among them. I realized what I had done—or more accurately, what I hadn't done. I felt shattered.

That event happened more than two decades ago, but to this day, I can't get Richard's face out of my memory. If I had initiated a conversation about Christ, he may have ignored my attempts to witness to him. But if I had heeded the voice of the Holy Spirit, he would have had a chance to alter his eternal destiny.

I learned a very difficult—and costly—lesson that day. I came face to face with the fact that ministry isn't about a place or a people group or a position. It's about simple and swift obedience to the One who called me in the first place. Though I have led others

to the Lord in the twenty-three years since then, I will always regret
the day I disobeyed.

LaVonna

If you want to get to the end of your life without regrets, there's only one way: be disciplined and determined to practice immediate obedience.

God rewards those who have a tender heart and a repentant spirit. However, some people remark, "I know people who use and abuse others and don't seem to feel guilty at all. In fact, they're proud of their power of intimidation!" Yes, virtually all of us know someone who can lie, cheat, steal, and hurt others, apparently without a shred of remorse. Those people are somewhere on the continuum of personality disorders. They may lean toward being sociopaths, narcissists, or victims of some other significant disorder. To some extent, they have "arrested moral development," so they aren't interested in humility, kindness, mercy, and submission to God. We need to watch out for them, guard ourselves against them, and refuse to let them keep us from fully following Christ.[15]

PARTIAL OBEDIENCE IS DISOBEDIENCE

The classic biblical example of partial obedience is King Saul's failure to fulfill God's command. Through Samuel, the Lord told Saul to attack the Amalekites and "destroy everything"—and He made it clear that He meant *everything*! Saul led his army and attacked. After the victorious battle, Samuel found Saul after he had erected a monument "in his own honor." Before the prophet could say a word, Saul announced, "The Lord bless you! I have carried out the Lord's instructions."

Samuel wasn't naïve. He knew Saul hadn't fully followed God's command because on his way to the camp he had already seen and heard the captured livestock. The prophet responded, "What then is this bleating of sheep in my ears? What is this lowing of cattle that I hear?"

Saul quickly blamed his men and even tried to put a religious spin on his disobedience: "The soldiers brought them from the Amalekites; they spared the best of the sheep and cattle to sacrifice to the Lord your God, but we totally destroyed the rest."

In spite of Samuel's repeated attempts to make Saul see his error, the king kept insisting he was blameless. Exasperated, Samuel finally pronounced God's judgment on Saul's partial obedience:

> "Does the LORD delight in burnt offerings and sacrifices as much as in obeying the LORD? To obey is better than sacrifice, and to heed is better than the fat of rams. For rebellion is like the sin of divination, and arrogance like the evil of idolatry. Because you have rejected the word of the LORD, he has rejected you as king" (1 Sam. 15:22–23).

Did King Saul obey God? He attacked the enemy, didn't he? He won the battle. Wasn't that a sign of God's approval? But Saul wasn't willing to do all God commanded him to do. He thought he had a better plan. God and the prophet Samuel weren't impressed with Saul's partial obedience.

If you tell your child to pick up his clothes and make his bed, but he only makes his bed, that's disobedience. If a student is assigned to read twenty pages in her history textbook, but she reads only fifteen pages, she's disobedient. If a businessman is required to make ten calls, but quits after making six, he's irresponsible and disobedient. When God puts it in my heart to give a waitress $100, if I only give her $50, I am disobedient.

Complete obedience tests our resolve.

Complete obedience tests our resolve. For example, when God tells us to care for annoying people, it can test our patience. Dr. Pat Knott is a physician who runs a rehabilitation clinic. She learned that the proof of her love for Jesus means going out of her way to show love. She discovered partial obedience isn't enough.

Pastor Rod,

The story I am about to tell does not show me in a very good light, but God spoke and I learned a valuable lesson.

I admitted a patient to the hospital about two years into my medical practice. This patient (about seventy-five years old) had chronic medical issues, one of which was COPD, which is like asthma. Each morning she would start to tell me about her medical complaints for the day, which is what I want my patients to do. The problem was that she would voice the same complaint every day, which consisted of her symptoms of COPD, what her medicines were, and how she thought she should take them. She had a long list of symptoms and meds, so this would take a good deal of time.

Due to the nature of my practice, I spent long periods of time on the unit, and every time this patient passed me in the hallway she would stop me and start over again about her meds.

I began to dodge this lady as much as possible. I would duck behind a wall if I saw her coming. The nurses even got in on it and warned me when she was approaching. Sometimes they would make up excuses about needing my attention on other matters just to "save me."

After this went on for a while, my behavior gradually started to prick my conscience. I didn't like how I was acting, and I also felt a bit of guilt that I, a leader in the hospital, was setting a bad example for the staff—not to mention, it was a very un-Christian example.

One evening after a long day at work, I was sitting at home during my quiet time, but couldn't seem to concentrate. Finally I said, "Okay, God. I can't continue to act the way I have with my patient, but You are going to have to help me, because I can't get anything done otherwise. I don't know what else to do. I need You to tell me what I can do to make this work!"

Almost immediately, the words "fifteen minutes" came to mind, followed by, "Give her fifteen minutes each morning." I thought, "That's a good idea, God! I'll just tell her that ten minutes every morning belongs to her. I'll let her tell me anything she wants to tell me uninterrupted."

Again, immediately God spoke to my spirit, "I said fifteen."

I pretty much threw up my hands, "Okay, God. Fifteen it is."

The next morning I saw her in the dining area and told her that I was going to make my rounds to see the other patients, but I would meet her in her room at 8:00. From 8:00 to 8:15 would be her time every morning to meet with me and tell me whatever she wanted me to know.

I entered her room at precisely 8:00, and for the first time since she was admitted, she had to search for something to talk about! We ended up discussing family, friends, and ideas. She had a great sense of humor! I don't recall her asking about her meds.

Each morning as I started rounds in the dining area, she sat at her table with a satisfied smile and left me alone. I would nod to acknowledge that I would see her at 8:00. Every morning until her discharge, we would talk for fifteen minutes. Sometimes we discussed medical issues, but mostly we discovered each other. I came to realize that she was anxious and lonely, but once she knew I would listen attentively to her every day, it reassured her and made her feel significant. Me? I learned a lesson in obedience and compassion. I also gained a friend.

Pat

DELAYED OBEDIENCE

More than anyone I've ever known, my father responded quickly to God's voice. It was the habit of a lifetime, and it was never drudgery. My dad saw his relationship with God as the biggest thrill and greatest adventure of his life. He believed he had an intimate relationship with someone who was braver than a SEAL, wiser than Socrates, and kinder than Mother Teresa. When he heard God speak to him, he was ready to move!

When God speaks to us, quite often our response is, "I will, God, but first . . ." We're not alone. Jesus met two men who proclaimed their allegiance to Him, but they wanted to wait before they acted. Luke describes the conversations:

> "[Jesus] said to another man, 'Follow me.' But he replied, 'Lord, first let me go and bury my father.' Jesus said to him, 'Let the dead bury their own dead, but you go and proclaim the kingdom of God.' Still another said, 'I will follow you, Lord; but first let me go back and say goodbye to my family.' Jesus replied, 'No one who puts a hand to the plow and looks back is fit for service in the kingdom of God'" (Luke 9:59–62).

Everything in our modern lives is orchestrated to provide convenience, and we assume God should be on our schedule, too. He's not. We're on His. Delay is costly. I've seen people shake their heads when they realize their reticence has caused them to miss out on God's best. They complain, "I knew God wanted me to share Christ with a friend (or give money or time or compassion), but I wanted to find a better time." I've talked to a number of people who were sure God had called them to full-time ministry, but they responded, "Great, but not yet. I want to do this or that first." For many of them, "this or that" became the focus of their lives, and they never followed through with their original intention to answer God's call. For many years, they live with nagging regrets. Delayed obedience inevitably leads to sad stories.

GOD'S DISCIPLINE

I know I would get an argument from a lot of children, but being disciplined by a parent isn't the worst thing that can happen to them. Far worse is when a parent is so disinterested in a child's life that he or she *doesn't* discipline the youngster when he needs it.

In His great love, God steps in to discipline His children. Often discipline is simply instruction to make naïve kids wise. But of course, when God's children go beyond naïveté to genuine foolishness, they need correction for their own good. King Solomon challenges us to appreciate the times when God steps in to change the direction of our lives: "My son, do not despise the LORD's discipline, and do not resent his rebuke, because the LORD disciplines those he loves, as a father the son he delights in" (Prov. 3:11–12).

God doesn't want us to let disobedience destroy our relationships, our finances, our health, and our futures. So as a loving, attentive, wise parent, He gets involved.

No good parent always rescues kids from suffering the consequences of their disobedience. We call that *enabling* or *codependent*. Part of God's (and any good parent's) discipline is to let disobedient children experience the consequences of poor choices. Quite often, that's the only way they will learn.

HOW LONG?

People sometimes ask me, "Pastor, how long will the consequences of disobedience last?" That's a good question, and it doesn't have a simple answer. We may not be able to abbreviate the impact of a sin we have committed. The gravity of some of our dumb choices stays with us the rest of our lives.

However, I would focus on a different consequence: missing the delight of God. The consequence of missing God's heart lasts as long as you remain defiant, disinterested, and disobedient. Yet as soon as you turn back to Him, you have the assurance that He welcomes you with open arms. You can't change the past, and you may not be able to do anything about the consequences of previous choices, but you can change direction today. The Bible calls this decision *repentance.*

Feeling bad isn't the solution. Remorse is not repentance. We feel remorse because we're sorry we got caught and we hate the pain we have inflicted on ourselves. Remorse leads directly to self-pity, which in sensitive people may also lead to self-hatred: "How could I have been so stupid?" The goal of remorse is to escape the consequences.

Repentance is categorically different. We're not just sorry we broke the rules; we're sorry because we broke God's heart. We don't blame others, and we don't make excuses. The Spirit of God (or a spouse, child, friend, or police officer) shines a light on our sin, and we own it: "Guilty as charged." We own it, but we don't wallow in it. We don't let shame trap us in a lifestyle of self-condemnation and continued disobedience. And we don't try to only "feel bad enough long enough" to pay for our sin so we can feel better. Instead, we turn to God and accept the forgiveness Christ has already purchased for us on the cross. Instead of being defiant or ashamed, we're deeply humbled that God would love us so much to forgive and restore us. We feel joy and gratitude instead of shame.

Part of repentance is a change of actions. We evaluate what led to the sin, and we take corrective measures. We change what we read, what we listen to, what we watch, whom we hang out with, and how we spend our time and money.

Disobedience closes doors of opportunity, but sometimes the door remains wide open to go back and obey God. When I realize I have failed to respond to God's leading, I pray three things:

- "Lord, forgive me for not responding to You."

- "Please give me another opportunity to obey you in this situation."

- "If that's not possible, would You send someone who is obedient to accomplish Your purposes."

> Life change requires dependence on God's love, the Holy Spirit's power, rigorous honesty, support from mature believers, and incredible tenacity.

Quite often, we need to change more than an isolated action; we need to change a destructive habit of a lifetime. Life change requires dependence on God's love, the Holy Spirit's power, rigorous honesty, support from mature believers, and incredible tenacity. If we think it will somehow "just happen," we will be deeply disappointed. When a person confesses to me that he's an addict, I ask, "What's your addiction? Tell me about it." The person then describes the substance or behavior. Then I ask, "Do you still crave it?"

Honest people say, "Yes, Pastor. Every single day."

I love it when people are brutally realistic about the mountain they need to climb. I tell them, "You're right where God wants you to be. We'll help you in every way we can, but it's up to you to obey God and create new habits."

I regularly talk to one young man in recovery for drugs, and I encourage him to keep walking with God to build a new life of faith, hope, and love. Recently I told him, "Don't quit before the new habits take root." He smiled and nodded. Then I added, "If you do, I'll hunt you down. I'll find you out on the street, and I'll drag you back to the recovery group and your sponsor." From the look on his face, he knew I wasn't kidding. That's what it means to love an addict.

THE FATHER'S HEART

Some of us have it all wrong about God. We assume He is just waiting for us to mess up so He can blast us. Jesus' parable of the two brothers (Luke 15) provides a very different perspective. The father in the story represents God. While the younger son wastes his fortune and his health in sin, the father longs for his return. When he sees his beloved boy on the road to the house, he does something most Middle Eastern patriarchs would never do: he hikes up his robe and runs to greet him! The delighted dad interrupts the boy's confession to assure the son of his love and welcome him back to the family. To celebrate, he throws the biggest party the town has ever seen!

The story, though, doesn't stop there. The older son has stayed home and worked hard for the father, but he hasn't enjoyed knowing and loving him. He's furious that his dad has welcomed the prodigal home, and he refuses to attend the party. The story ends with the father graciously going out to the field to tenderly invite the angry, defiant son to join the feast.

In both cases—with the wild, crazy, sinning son as well as the furious, self-righteous one—the father compassionately and assertively invites the child to enjoy his warmth and blessings. That's a picture of God's desire to welcome us, too. Whether we've been like the younger brother or the elder brother, we can be sure God longs to shower us with forgiveness and acceptance. When we show up, He celebrates!

Painful consequences can result from our sins or the sins of another—and often a combination of both. Even when Carol felt she was beyond hope, God showed up in His love and strength.

> *Pastor Rod,*
>
> *My marriage was breaking apart. I made a mistake in keeping that from my family, hoping I could hide the fact that I was living with an abuser. I thought, for years, that I could find some magic fix and not be the first one in my family to get a divorce. I had been less than honest with my parents, in particular, so the news of my failing marriage was a shock to them.*
>
> *I had come from Mississippi to Arkansas to stay with my parents for a few days. My dad is a pastor, and he tried to fix what was irretrievably broken. I had finally told them I was being abused, but I had glossed over it.*

My dad was adamant about my giving my spouse another chance. I knew the consequences of going back, but I had just about given up at this point. After years of crying out to God, fasting, praying, attending church, and doing everything else "right," I just didn't care anymore, and I was convinced God was deaf when it came to me.

Mom, Dad, and I loaded up for the return trip to Mississippi. Dad was going to drive me down so he could talk with my husband. He hoped to work things out between us.

We drove as far as a little café in East Arkansas, where Dad pulled over. He told Mom and me to go in and get coffee. Through the window, Mom and I watched in confusion as Dad walked around the parking lot, appearing to talk to himself. After about twenty minutes, Dad came in and told Mom, "We can't go. We can't take her back to him."

We wondered what had happened. Dad explained that he had felt God strongly tell him to pull over and get out of the truck. He then began praying in the parking lot. He said God clearly told him, "If you leave her, the next time you see her will be in a casket."

We returned to my parents' home. I truly believe my Dad's immediate obedience saved my life—and I know it changed mine.

I wasn't necessarily angry at God. I had just given up on Him because I figured He had given up on me. I knew going back to Mississippi would be bad for my health, but I was beyond caring. When God stopped my dad, it proved that God hadn't given up on me.

I'll never be proud of my failed marriage, but I know that God
saw me even in my failures and rescued me.

Carol

CONSIDER THIS . . .

1. Do you agree or disagree with the statement: "Disobedience never
    leads to good results." Explain your answer. What are some reasons
    people think it's a better way?

2. When disobedient people resent that God blesses obedient people,
    what do you imagine they're thinking? How does their anger make
    sense to them? How would you help them see the truth about the
    connection between obedience and God's blessings?

3. How have you seen disobedience spread like a virus to other parts
    of a person's life?

4. What's the problem with partial and delayed obedience? Why
    doesn't God grade on a curve and accept it?

5. How do you view God's discipline? Do you despise it or welcome
    it? Explain your answer.

6. If someone asked you, "How long will the consequences of disobe-
    dience last?" what would you tell him?

7. Define and describe repentance. How is it different from remorse?

8. Why is it important to realize that sin isn't just breaking God's rules,
    but breaking His heart? How would this insight help you respond
    to His discipline?

7

LESSONS LEARNED

"God is constantly on the move. I cannot stay where I am and follow God
at the same time; responding requires movement."
—Margaret Feinberg

The first year I began to practice immediate obedience, I discovered a new dimension to spiritual life. It had been there all along, and I had tasted it many times, but I began to drink from a fire hose! After a month or so, I got up every day wondering what God might say to me that day. I might not hear anything, or I might get a word from Him to step into someone's life. I began to see myself as "on call," like a soldier or like an EMS doctor or nurse. When I got the call, I was ready! And I've never been disappointed.

Of course, tapping into the mind and heart of God is both a thrill and a challenge. I never know what God might say, but His character is always awesome and His ways are inscrutable. I've been on an adventure, and I love it. During that first year, I often obeyed even when I saw no observable result. But sometimes the impact was visible and immediate.

One night I had arranged for a missionary to speak to us in our church service. We always ask our people to give to the projects we present, but as this man spoke, I clearly sensed God telling me to change the plan. When the missionary finished, I got up and told our congregation, "Our church is going to support him and his project, but the offering tonight isn't about that. I believe God wants us to help his daughter go to college. The money you give tonight will go toward her tuition and expenses."

Our people gave generously. A few days later, the man called to tell me that at the moment I asked people to give, his daughter was crying because the family couldn't afford to send her to college. God's clear message to me was to enlist our church to partner with this dear family to send a daughter to college. The money we gave covered all her expenses for a full year.

I want to briefly describe some more of the wonderful lessons I learned that first year—and that I'm continuing to learn every day.

THE MORE WE LISTEN, THE MORE WE HEAR

With practice, my spiritual ears became increasingly sensitive to God's voice. When I read the Scriptures, it became more than merely maintaining a spiritual discipline. More than ever, I expected the Spirit to illumine my mind to grasp God's truth and hear His voice. As I prayed, I wasn't just going through the motions. I saw prayer as a two-way communication. I made sure to leave time to listen as well as praise God and make requests. Sometimes I didn't sense anything beyond God's smile, and to be honest, that's more than enough! But often, God broke in to give me clear directions to take a step of obedience that day. And I learned that hearing God isn't limited to "special times" of Bible study and prayer. I live in God's presence all day, every day. He is omni-present; I'm never apart from Him. I gradually became more aware that He could speak to me about anything at any time.

These insights weren't new theological truths. I had known them for many years. But in my initial year of radical obedience, I began to put them into practice in ways I had never done before.

THE DIVINE AMONG THE ORDINARY

In the year of learning to hear God and instantly obey Him, I discovered an important truth. I looked in the mirror and realized God—in His grace and humor—delights to use very ordinary people. People like me.

God isn't looking for superstars. The people who responded to Jesus were fishermen, laborers, hated tax collectors, prostitutes, the blind, the lame, and the outcasts. A few noble people, like Joseph of Arimathea, were in the mix, but not many. At the incarnation, Jesus was born to a peasant couple. That night the angels appeared to shep-herds, not kings or generals. The angel didn't tell the shepherds to look in a palace for the newborn King. He told them to look in an animal feeding trough!

If you're ordinary, you're just the person God is looking for!

It's not only ordinary *people* that God works through; it's also in ordinary *times*. I'm afraid some pastors and church leaders insinu-ate that the presence of God is more real during the hour or so in the church building every Sunday morning. It's not. When Jesus died on the cross, a stunning event happened a few blocks away. Mark tells us,

"The curtain of the temple was torn in two from top to bottom" (Mark 15:38). For centuries, the curtain had separated the Holy of Holies, where the glory of God dwelled, from the outside world. But when Jesus died, God supernaturally ripped the curtain and His almighty presence became available to every person who believes.

Does God speak to people in church services? I sure hope so! But He also speaks when you're stuck in traffic, changing diapers, having coffee with a friend, relaxing, alone, or in a crowd. The curtain is open. God's glory—His tender and fierce presence—is with you all day every day in every activity of your life. God wants to speak to you in the ordinary moments of your life . . . if you will just listen.

PERFECT TIMING

During my first year of immediate obedience, I began to notice that God put people and situations together in exquisite timing. It was like watching an NFL quarterback throw a pass to a receiver on a crossing pattern. We marvel at the quarterback's skill when the ball arrives in exactly the right place at exactly the right time. Far more, we marvel when we realize God has orchestrated events and people to accomplish what only He can do.

Have you ever wondered about those stories where God breaks into a person's consciousness and gives directions to pray for a missionary at the precise moment the missionary's life is in danger? I'm convinced God prompts the person to pray at that precise moment. But God orchestrates His perfect timing for everybody, not just missionaries. Sherry told me about God's perfect timing in an awkward relationship:

Pastor,

Bob and I had been divorced several years. The boys were grown, and I didn't have to communicate with him very much. Our relationship was okay. I had forgiven him, but I still didn't like him or trust him. To be honest, I didn't even want to think about him.

One night God woke me up and said very plainly, "Pray for Bob." I hoped I was dreaming. I tried to go back to sleep, but two more times God said, "Pray for Bob." I looked at the ceiling and told God, "Are you kidding? Why would I want to do that?" I turned over and tried to go back to sleep. God began to remind me, "Bob is your son's dad, he needs salvation, and he needs protection." At that point, I began to pray sincerely. The next morning nothing special happened, and I had no idea why God had spoken.

About three years later, Bob and I were on much friendlier terms. One day he told me about a wreck he had been involved in three years earlier. He had been driving an eighteen-wheeler that ran into the back of another eighteen-wheeler, totaling his truck and trailer. Bob was trapped under the steering wheel until a rescue team got him out. He said a State Trooper had told him he shouldn't have made it out alive.

As he described the event, I thought, "Hmm. Could that have been the night . . . ?" I asked him to tell me the date and time it happened. It was the exact moment God woke me up and told me to pray for him!

I told him, "Well you may not believe this, but God woke me up that night and told me to pray for you."

He said, "God must have answered your prayers because I'm still alive." I also told him I had asked God why I had to pray for him. He got a laugh out of that.

Sherry

When you practice immediate obedience, God will use you at exactly the right moment. His timing is impeccable.

I can't tell you how often people tell me, "Pastor, when you said that today, it was exactly what I needed to hear. And I needed to hear it today! God really spoke to me through your message." Sometimes a particular point, story, or principle had been in my notes for weeks, but I had overlooked it until that day. Other times, I sensed something at the moment and determined to be obedient. Either way, God knew when it needed to be shared and who needed to hear it.

One of my biggest challenges at first was trying to figure out what God was up to. Occasionally I sensed God putting in my heart to ask people if they were ready to accept Jesus, but the moment seemed completely wrong. To me, it made absolutely no sense. But I was learning to be immediately obedient, so I went for it.

On those occasions (and many others), I thought, *If no one responds, I'm going to look really stupid!* But I didn't let my fear keep me from obeying. Every time, God was designing the precise moment for the person sitting before me. I may not have been ready, but God and the person were! I'm so glad I obeyed.

Pastors haven't cornered the market on God's timing. He wants to use you for divine moments in His divine timing! As you obey Him immediately, you'll be amazed how many times He leads you to do or say exactly what is needed at precisely the right time.

One day a year or so ago, I was struggling with discouragement. I know all the passages about trusting God in hard times, but I'm thoroughly human. Sometimes I struggle to find hope—especially when someone I love is turning his back on God. On that day, I was thinking about a person in whom I had invested a lot of love and time. I thought he had been making progress, but the latest report was very discouraging. At the moment of my deepest anguish, Bev Cooper sent me an email. It was a prayer for my family and me, filled with specific, God-inspired encouragement! Through that email, God spoke words of hope to my heart at the exact moment I needed to hear from Him.

Actually, I experienced God's perfect timing several times that first year. At the precise moment when I was being criticized or attacked, God used a person in our church to speak words of encouragement and direction in my life. God knew where I was and used my friends to minister to me. To them, it must have seemed out of the blue. To me, it was God's perfect message in His perfect time.

It can happen on any day at any moment:

God knows what's going on in your waitress' life, and He wants to use you to meet her needs.

God knows your boss' problems and what he needs to hear, and He wants to use you to encourage him.

God knows about the student who is ready to commit suicide, and He wants to send you with the right words at the right time.

God knows about the guy who's trying to decide whether to give up on his marriage. God will send you with a word of hope at precisely the right moment.

Divine appointments and divine timing are no coincidence when you're committed to obeying God immediately! Seeing God use you in this way will be your greatest adventure.

Open your heart and mind to the possibility that God wants to interrupt your daily agenda with supernatural, divine encounters. You don't have to understand all the what's, why's, and how's. God is the sovereign King of the universe. He knows what He's doing! You may not grasp a billionth of a zillionth of what He's up to, yet it's your incredible privilege that He invites you to be His child and His partner in redeeming the world. You can trust in His leading even when you don't understand it, and you can trust in His timing even when it makes no sense to you.

People can have expectations of spiritual life that are too high or too low. Both extremes can create problems. The Bible paints a glowing picture of our new identity and our new relationship with God. We are God's adopted children who can go boldly to His throne with our requests. In Israel, the temple was where heaven and earth intersected; now *we* are temples of the Holy Spirit—the presence of God resides in us (1 Cor. 6:19–20)!

God has given us a taste of His glory, His heart, His purposes, and His mind, but we haven't yet experienced our full transformation. Jesus' resurrection is the "firstfruits," but our resurrection will surely follow

(1 Cor. 15:23). That's His promise and our hope. He gave us the Holy Spirit as a "deposit" or "down payment" of what's to come when we meet Jesus face to face (Eph. 1:13–14). In this life, we experience both groaning and glory (Rom. 8:22–25, 31–39). We are in touch with the Creator of the universe, but for now we only see but a poor reflection as in a mirror (1 Cor. 13:12).

So we shouldn't be surprised if and when we get confused. God is doing something far, far bigger than anything we can imagine. Solomon eloquently described the paradox in which we live as flawed and limited people in touch with the perfect God: "[God] has made everything beautiful in its time. He has also set eternity in the human heart; yet no one can fathom what God has done from beginning to end" (Ecc. 3:11). As we listen for God's voice, our hearts swell with joy that He calls us His own, but they are also humbled when we realize our transformation is still very much in process.

Immediate obedience is the readiness to be "on call" and move as soon as we hear God's voice. In His eyes, the "right time" may be for our benefit, or it may be for the other person's benefit. Either way, we know God's timing is best.

> Immediate obedience is the readiness to be "on call" and move as soon as we hear God's voice.

Believe He wants to use you to speak or give precisely what people need at the exact time they need it. There's no arrogance in this way of thinking because we realize we could never pull this off on our own!

THE REAL HERO

During the first year of my immediate obedience adventure, I had many opportunities to take credit for the amazing things that happened. When I'm obedient and God uses me to touch someone's life, the person often sees *me* as the source of blessing. It's entirely understandable . . . and entirely wrong. I redirect the person to the ultimate source and give glory to God. When someone thanks me, I often say, "Oh, it's my privilege. The thanks go to God. He knows you, and He knows what you need. He loves you so much that He prompted me to be His hands and voice to communicate that love. I was just being obedient to Him."

That's the pattern of Scripture. Jesus lived to glorify the Father, and the Spirit glorifies the Father and the Son. Paul—probably the greatest and most gifted leader the world has ever known, apart from Jesus— was careful to always deflect honor away from himself to God. At one point in his travels, Paul healed a crippled man. The crowd was amazed. Luke tells us, "They shouted in the Lycaonian language, 'The gods have come down to us in human form!' Barnabas they called Zeus, and Paul they called Hermes because he was the chief speaker. The priest of Zeus, whose temple was just outside the city, brought bulls and wreaths to the city gates because he and the crowd wanted to offer sacrifices to them'" (Acts 14:11–13).

Imagine being mistaken for the top Greek gods! People were so impressed they wanted to sacrifice sacred bulls to Paul and Barnabas. But the two men would have nothing of it. They practiced immediate obedience by redirecting attention to the true source of healing power.

Luke continues, "But when the apostles Barnabas and Paul heard of this, they tore their clothes and rushed out into the crowd, shouting: 'Friends, why are you doing this? We too are only men, human, like you. We are bringing you good news, telling you to turn from these worthless things to the living God, who made the heavens and the earth and the sea and everything in them'" (Acts 14:14–15).

If our motive is God's glory, we won't desire applause, and if we get it, we'll make sure to point people to God. If your motive is selfish, then you'll give up when you don't get immediate results. And actually, the consequences could be worse . . . much worse.

In an incident that occurred shortly before this incident with Paul and Barnabas, a crowd in Caesarea tried to flatter King Herod by equating him with a god. The historian Josephus tells us that Herod wore a robe made of silver that sparkled in the sun.[16] Luke also describes the event. When Herod spoke, the crowds yelled, "This is the voice of a god, not of a man." Herod didn't deny it, but basking in the glow of glory was costly for the king. We read that, "Immediately, because Herod did not give praise to God, an angel of the Lord struck him down, and he was eaten by worms and died" (Acts 12:22–23). Herod wanted to be a hero, but he died a fool.

The moral of the story is clear and powerful: God is the only one who deserves glory. We have a choice: to call attention to who we are and what we have done, or to

We have a choice: to call attention to who we are and what we have done, or to call attention to our King and Savior.

call attention to our King and Savior. If we choose to honor ourselves, we probably won't be eaten by worms, but our hearts will be eaten by comparison, competition, jealousy, pride, and fear. Make the right call. Choose to give glory to God.

Almost every time we obey by caring for someone, we have the opportunity to give glory to God. One day at a restaurant, I overheard a girl ordering lunch in the line next to me. She kept asking for prices of the menu items, trying to find a combination she could afford. After several of her attempts had failed, it was becoming clear she didn't have enough money for lunch at this place, so I told the person behind the register, "I want to pay for hers."

I turned to the young lady and smiled, "What would you like? It's on me today."

She looked at me in shock and placed her order. She turned back to me and said, "Thanks."

The girl behind the register didn't know what to think. She told me, "That was so cool. I can't believe it."

I answered, "Just a little kindness from God. I'm only the messenger."

How did God use that act of immediate obedience? I have no idea. It might have been for the girl who was hungry. It might have been for the girl behind the register. It might have been for me. I'll probably never know for sure, but that's fine with me. It's not about my being a hero; it's about God receiving glory.

In his classic book, *Spiritual Leadership*, Oswald Sanders told the story of a nineteenth-century itinerant Scottish minister who found a practical way to give God glory instead of honoring himself. Sanders wrote, "When Robert Murray McCheyne experienced times of bless-ing in his ministry, on returning home from the service, he would kneel down and symbolically place the crown of success on the brow of the Lord to whom he knew it rightly belonged. This practice helped to save him from the peril of arrogating to himself the glory which belonged to God."[17]

It's an unspeakable honor that the God of heaven and earth is willing to involve me in His grand plans to save people and restore the world. Who am I that He would call me His child and partner? He's God. He doesn't need me or anyone else to rule the universe, but He has chosen to engage flawed, dense human beings like me to play a tiny role in accomplishing His grand plans. He could rain money out of the sky on those in need. He could speak through a donkey or a car horn to give people directions. But He has chosen me (and you, too) to join hands with Him. It's so amazing. It's so cool.

Do you want to experience the thrill of responding to the King and seeing Him use you? I know you do. Our willingness to redirect the glory to God is a test of our devotion. Like McCheyne, we can make the choice to honor God even when we would like to keep the credit. He deserves it; we don't. Give it all to Him.

I've known people who developed a Messiah complex as they helped others. They always made sure other people knew how much they had to suffer and sacrifice in order to be of help. Those misguided people aren't really serving God or the people in need. They're padding their own reputations.

Immediate obedience is countercultural. It's playing by a com-pletely different set of rules. In the Sermon on the Mount, Jesus described two diametrically different reasons to pray, give, and fast: to be noticed by people and win their applause, or purely for "your Father, who is unseen" (Matt. 6:2–18). It's human nature to want accolades, but a humble heart realizes we don't deserve them, so we learn to be content to serve quietly, even secretly, and always give God the credit.

People who seek prestige don't do anything in secret, and they can't wait to tell others about their successes. When God tells them to do something behind the scenes so that no one will notice, they chafe. When they see someone else get results by obeying God, they don't celebrate. Their spirit of competition creates resentment of others and anger toward God. Even when someone gives glory to God, they accuse the person of pride and arrogance. (Psychologists call this *projection*.) They keep trying to stay in the spotlight while others simply, and immediately, obey God.

As we develop the habit of listening to God and being immediately obedient, we can expect pride—our own and others'—to accuse and attack. The darkness of human nature is powerful, but God's love, grace, and power are far stronger. Fight the good fight. Choose to honor God at every step, and pray for those who don't understand. No matter what, keep listening and responding to God.

God will fulfill His purposes—with or without you. If you're insensitive to the Spirit or unresponsive when you hear God speak, God will find someone else. You aren't indispensable to His plans. He's incredibly creative and resourceful in accomplishing His purposes in the lives of people around you. It's your great privilege—not a right or entitlement—to take His hand and join Him in changing the world.

NOT POPULAR BUT RIGHT

Sometimes obeying God has led me to stand against evil and for justice, mercy, and truth—and those stands aren't always popular. I was in a contentious community leadership meeting when I felt God lead me to speak in support of a particular leader and his perspective. Powerful forces were lined up to oppose him. I knew my support would be costly, but I stood and spoke out for him.

After the meeting, I texted Cindy, "I just committed political and social suicide."

She immediately responded, "Was it right?"

I sent a quick reply, "Yes."

She wrote, "Then we'll survive. I'm with you."

God has called us to be salt and light in families, schools, businesses, clubs, politics, and church. We represent the hope of the world! But as we represent Christ, we become targets for those who don't share our values. Sometimes it can get extremely uncomfortable.

Biblical examples abound. God led Philip to go far out of his way to reach a foreigner, an Ethiopian eunuch who had been to the temple but was only admitted to the outer courts. Peter went to Cornelius's house and crossed lines of racial prejudice. Paul argued for Gentiles to be included as equal partners in God's church.

Jesus lived on the razor's edge of the Father's calling. The ultraconservative Pharisees felt threatened by His love for the unrighteous and His disregard for the petty rules they added to God's law. The liberal Sadducees despised Him because He kept pointing them to the Bible and reminding them that truth is more important than their modern notions. Those who followed King Herod were aghast when the crowds began to acknowledge Jesus as the true King. In the end, all three groups conspired to kill Him. If we stand for truth—and if we want to become more like Jesus—shouldn't we expect opposition from all sides?

When we practice immediate obedience, we may even experience opposition from those closest to us—members of our family. We can be kind, thoughtful, and gracious, yet some of those who know us best will be threatened by our allegiance to God. When we put Him first, they get upset. In one of His most chilling statements, Jesus gave us a heads-up: "Do not suppose that I have come to bring peace to the earth. I did not come to bring peace, but a sword. For I have come to turn 'a man against his father, a daughter against her mother, a daughter-in-law against her mother-in-law—a man's enemies will be the members of his own household'" (Matt. 10:34–36).

If you live wholeheartedly for Jesus Christ, it's possible that at least some people in your family will think you've lost your mind. Yet when they don't respond well to your spiritual growth, it's not a virtue to annoy them with rigid, heartless righteousness. Trying to force them to believe what you believe isn't the way of the cross. Insensitivity and obnoxiousness are not spiritual gifts.

In the family of God, it seems many people consider pastors and other church leaders to be fair game for attacks. For some strange reason, some people assume they have the right to dictate the policies, procedures, and personnel of their church. They don't just have opinions; they make demands! And when I don't comply with a person's requests (or expectations or demands), it can create conflict. People don't like it when they don't get their way. I try to be respectful of people's opinions, but I'm not living to please them. I want to please and obey God.

For anyone who will listen, let me share my perspective as a church leader. If you don't like something, or you think I'm wrong about something, please tell me—but tell me with a servant's heart. When suggestions are offered in the right spirit, I can more easily listen. God may use your observations and input to speak to me. But understand this: your preference isn't going to lead our church, and neither is mine. It's not about you, and it's not about me—it's about God.

People who determine to obey God should never be known for their anger and arrogance. Loving and obeying God don't produce a judgmental attitude, a critical spirit, or a negative, condescending treatment of others.

I can't tell you how many times people have said, in an angry and hateful way, "Pastor, God told me this or that." Their attitude reveals that God probably didn't tell them anything! They're just using His name to make their argument stronger.

Obeying God may create conflict, but the disputes should never arise from our bad attitude. Genuine obedience puts us in touch with His heart, His love, and His power—and that's what flows out of us into the lives of those around us. The more our hearts are in line with

God's, the more we will think, feel, and act like Jesus. His nature will seep into ours.

BE A CHEERLEADER

In my first year of immediate obedience, Cindy, Parker, Tyler, and a few others became cheerleaders as I told them stories of God speaking and my privilege of obeying Him. I realized all of us need cheerleaders. As parents, spouses, friends, and leaders, we need to create an environment that stimulates faith and celebrates obedience. Far too often, I've seen people take the first steps to respond immediately after hearing from God, only to have another person quickly throw a wet blanket of doubt on them. Instead of offering support, the other person sneers, "Oh, you can't be serious. That doesn't make any sense. Grow up. Life doesn't work that way."

We need to be one another's fans, celebrating *acts* of obedience, not *results* of obedience. I've heard people say that evangelism is sharing Christ in the power of the Spirit and leaving the results to God. Obedience is like that too: it's hearing God's whisper, responding in faith, and leaving the results to God. The results aren't a measurement of the value of a person's obedience. The obedience itself pleases God ... and if we're in tune with Him, it pleases us, too.

When Tyler told Cindy and me that he wanted to change his career plans, he wasn't sure we would be happy about the switch. We had been excited when he got a full scholarship to UALR, and we were very happy when he did so well in his first year. When he finally mustered the courage to tell us that God had put in his heart to go to Bible school and become a pastor, we were thrilled and Tyler was relieved. Together we celebrated his obedience.

We need to celebrate when our spouses and children actively listen to God and respond. We need to celebrate when a friend shares her fears about obeying but steps out in faith. We need to celebrate when young adults feel called to missions. We need to celebrate when people respond to God's summons to go to the most difficult nations and cultures on earth. We need to celebrate when an addict walks into a meeting and says, "My life's a wreck. I need help. I need God."

As a husband, father, and leader, it's my job and my joy to create an atmosphere where obedience to God's voice is celebrated. And it's your job to create the same kind of environment in your home.

Several years ago, Nathan Kollar, our church planter in Santa Monica, California, spoke on a Sunday night. After church, Parker came to me and said, "Dad, I need my money." I'm the bank for Cindy and the boys, not because they need any help, but because they can access it more quickly. Parker had been saving his money for a boat.

I asked him, "How much of your savings do you want to take out?"

He answered, "All of it."

I was surprised. I wondered if he had seen an ad for boats and was ready to get one. I asked, "What for, son?"

He replied, "God told me to give it to Nathan for the church."

I didn't argue with Parker. I knew he had heard from God, and he was obeying.

That night Parker gave Nathan a huge amount of money—everything he had. Cindy and I celebrated with Parker and talked about how

God would use the money to rescue people from hell and build disciples—the kind of disciples who will give generously when they hear God's voice. I can't tell you how many times Parker has emptied his wallet and given everything. I don't correct him and call him "irresponsible." I celebrate his tender heart and obedience! He inspires me.

Some kids grasp the concept of obedience more quickly and easily than adults do. When Anna approached her ninth birthday, she told her parents, "I don't want a party where people bring presents for me. I want to invite them to come so I can share the need for planting churches in Vietnam."

Anna sent out the invitations. A couple of weeks later, her friends and family came to the party. Instead of presents, they brought an offering. Anna gathered her friends together and read this letter to them:

> The reason I wanted to do this is because God has a challenge for us to reach the whole world and teach them about God and how God's Son died on the cross and rose again so we could have eternal life. If every Christian child gave up one birthday, the whole world would be reached. Thank you for coming and helping me raise money to build a church in Vietnam. Thank you for making my prayers and my wish come true!

Anna raised over $1,700 to plant a church in Vietnam! In fact, her money planted two. Imagine that: a nine year-old girl responded to the voice of God, and the Lord used her heart, her generosity, and her creativity to advance His kingdom half a world away!

PATTERNS

I saw definite patterns emerge as the year of immediate obedience progressed. I was usually sensitive and responsive when God told me to give money to people. I had seen my father give money away so often that giving was part of my DNA. But there were some holes. I had a hard time believing God might use delays to give me an opportunity to demonstrate His love.

Only days ago I was having lunch at a local restaurant. The waitress didn't seem particularly distressed in any way, but I sensed the Lord tell me to give her $100. During my first year, I had developed a statement to let people know *why* I was giving them money. After lunch, I handed the waitress a $100 bill, and I told her, "The Lord told me to give this to you. He wants you to know that He knows what's going on in your life. And He wants me to tell you that He loves you very much."

Instantly she took the bill, grasped my hands, and dissolved into tears. Through her sobs, she told me, "You have no idea what this means to me. Thank you so much!" I had a feeling she was talking more about the impact of the message than the money. I have to tell you: I love it when God works like that!

But I'm still learning, especially when it comes to frustrating times of waiting. At one point during my first year, I spoke at a church in Wisconsin. Afterward, Cindy and I were trying to get home, but bad weather had caused tremendous disruptions in flight schedules—as if it were easy to get from Wisconsin to Little Rock in the first place! We cancelled and rescheduled twelve different flights as we went to one city, then tried to find the best flight to the next and the next. We wanted to get as far as we could as fast as we could, but we weren't making much progress. It was terribly frustrating.

Late in the day, we were in Atlanta. All the passengers, baggage, and crew were on a plane scheduled to leave at 11:00 p.m. We sat for a while, and then they asked us to get off and wait in the gate area. At 1:00 in the morning, we heard the announcement that the flight was cancelled. The next available flight wasn't until 6:00.

I was stewing during the five hours I had to wait, but Cindy was making friends. I sat alone, but she forged a new relationship with a family from Little Rock. By the time we got on the plane, I realized I had missed a golden opportunity to be a source of light in a place darkened by frustration and resentment. I had missed it, but Cindy had seized it.

I'm still learning. Thank God He's so patient! I do better when God tells me to give money than when He tells me to overcome disappointing circumstances and connect with people. But at least I see the patterns so I can anticipate them.

AN EXPECTANT HEART

At the end of the year of immediate obedience, I knew my life would never be the same. I told God, "I want to live this way for the rest of my life. If anything, I want to become a much better listener, and I want to respond even more quickly." The lessons I learned that year were so freeing and energizing, I couldn't go back to the way I had been before.

I learned to live with an expectant heart. Every encounter, every meeting, every delay could be a divine moment when God would give me specific directions to step into a person's life to give him or her a taste of His love. It was so exciting! And it still is.

I'm so thankful for the people who have joined me on this journey of hearing God and answering with glad obedience. We're in it together. It's a wonderful ride. Living with the expectation that at any moment I might hear God's voice makes life a lot of fun!

CONSIDER THIS . . .

1. How is learning to hear God's voice like learning to play a sport or a musical instrument?

2. As you've read the book so far, can you tell that you're more sensitive to God's whispers and nudges? Explain your answer.

3. Why is it important to realize there are no spiritual superstars and that God delights in using ordinary people to do extraordinary things?

4. Is giving God glory a choice or an instinctive response of humility? Explain your answer. What happens to our hearts when we take the credit?

5. When is standing up for God popular? When does it create waves (in families, businesses, politics, clubs, and churches)?

6. What difference does it make when people celebrate obedience in your life? Who are the people whose obedience you can cheer?

7. In what areas (money, delays, kindness to strangers, service, etc.) are you typically responsive to God's voice? In what areas do you need some work?

8

GETTING (AND STAYING) ALIGNED WITH GOD

"God loves to pour out His Spirit with power on those who will dare to align radically their purposes with His."

—*Steve Childers*

E ven a slight miscalculation in the trajectory of a missile can cause widespread panic—or disaster. The United States military has spent billions to perfect the guidance systems on rockets. They know that if the trajectory is off by a tiny fraction of a degree, the missile will land many miles from the intended target.

In our lives, the principle is equally true: when the initial trajectory is off even by a seemingly small amount, the landing point can be miles from our target of God's glory and our joy, freedom, fulfillment, and effectiveness. Our decisions today affect our ability to obey tomorrow. Today's choices open doors or close them, lead toward the fulfillment of God's desires for us or create barriers.

I know a young man who feels God has called him to the mission field, but five years ago he began incurring student loans. So far he hasn't found a way to pay down the debt, so his answer to God's calling is, "Yes, I want to, but I can't right now." In the years it will take him to pay off the loans, we'll see if he remains dedicated to God's leading and lives a frugal life of tenacious faith, or if he begins the incremental process of buying and borrowing more. The jury is out . . . and it will be for several years.

The problem isn't always the lack of finances. Sometimes the limitation is the lure of a comfortable life. I know a young man who told me several years ago that God had called him to spend more time with his wife and kids. He said, "I'm looking forward to that, but I just got promoted at my company. I'm making more money than I ever dreamed I would make! If I stay here a few more years, my family will have a cushion. Then I'll have more free time to spend with them." He missed the point. God has already told him what to do, and He is the only cushion the young man and his family needs. As long as he is focused on his career and income, his wife and kids *feel* neglected—because they *are* neglected.

Quite often, the inability to follow God's leading today is the result of poor financial decisions. With deep sadness, people have told me:

"I know God wants me to do that, but I can't afford it."

"I want to obey God, but I've got this house payment (or car payment or student loan payment)."

"I know God is calling me to be a missionary, but I can't leave my job."

"I'd like to plant a church, but I need a bigger salary than what
the church is offering."

Sometimes reluctance is based on relationships that are more
important than God and His will.

"I know God is speaking to me, but my husband (or wife) isn't
willing to make some hard decisions about where He might
lead us."

"I'm devoting myself completely to my children. At this point,
they really need me. Maybe someday I'll have more time to
give to God."

"I'd like to pastor a church, but my parents would be really
upset. They want me to have a comfortable life."

These sad conversations include the same two components: people
have a clear sense of God speaking to them, but they face a barrier or an
excuse that prevents them from following Him.

When we realize our "life guidance system" is out of alignment
with God's will, we have a choice. We can decide to pursue God with all
our hearts, or we can give up in despair and live a second-rate life. The
good news is that no matter how terrible our previous decisions have
been, God is always ready to lift us out of the quagmire. He is the God
of second chances (and third and fourth).

If you're a young person, you have the opportunity to set the trajectory of your life so that your purpose and direction align with God's.

If you're older and have made some bad choices (and who hasn't?), all hope isn't lost. You can make mid-course corrections—and you can warn others not to make the same mistakes you've made. If you'll repent and turn to Him, God promises not to waste your pain or your mistakes. You can learn incredible lessons about His mercy, and you can be a beacon of truth and hope to those around you.

Recently a young woman came to my office with some good news. She is a mom with a part-time job, and her husband makes a modest salary. For years, they lived under the crushing weight of credit card debt. They assumed their lives would always be clouded by debt, but then they heard about the possibility of realignment and transformation. They began making hard choices. After several years, she came to my office and announced, "Pastor Rod, yesterday we paid off our last credit card bill. We're no longer in debt! We can finally do whatever God calls us to do whenever He speaks to us. I'm so excited I can't stand it!"

No matter where you are in your trajectory, you have some very clear choices of alignment (or realignment). Don't put them off. Waiting won't make them easier. You'll be glad you delayed the hard but necessary decisions to put yourself in a position to answer when God speaks.

FIRST, THE HEART

The prerequisite of spiritual alignment isn't about money or time or relationships. It's about God. If our hearts aren't His, our choices will be self-serving. We have to be ruthlessly honest about the attraction of things that are second best. It's not a sin to have nice things, positions of power, a measure of comfort, or the admiration of our friends—but it's a sin to love any of those things more than God.

> The prerequisite of spiritual alignment isn't about money or time or relationships. It's about God.

When anything or anyone is more important to us than God, it has become an idol. How can we tell? First, we can look at our desires. What are the longings that capture our minds when we have free time? Do we daydream about having a bigger boat, a fabulous vacation, the applause of friends, or a promotion to the next rung up at the company? Or do our minds drift toward the amazing love of God for us? We can also look at our reactions when we don't get something we hoped for. Do we respond in anger, blame, and deep despair? Or do we hold those positions, possessions, and popularity loosely because we have experienced "the surpassing worth of knowing Christ my Lord" (Phil. 3:8–9)? Whatever defines our identity and gives us ultimate meaning and security is our god. If it's not the only true God, we're already out of alignment before we make a single choice.

In *Desiring God's Will*, author David Benner observes, "While the choices we make can be very important in our spiritual journey, we [see] that how we decide can often be as important as what we decide. Willpower, determination, and discipline are not enough in Christ-following. The close interconnection of will and desire means that if Christ is to have our will, he must first have our heart."[18]

ALIGNED TO SAY YES TO GOD

Strategically and intentionally, make decisions today that will allow you to say "yes, Lord" tomorrow. Do everything you can so you'll never have to say to God, "I'd like to obey, but I can't."

I know a couple who lived for twenty years at the edge of their income. With each promotion and raise, they bought a little bigger house and a little nicer car, and they went on a little better vacation. Eventually they realized they were fitting into the world's mold of values, and it was time to conform to God's priorities. They sold their big, fine home and moved their family into a more modest house. They gave away a significant portion of the profits, but they kept some so they would be ready and able when God told them to use it for His kingdom. They were now aligned to say yes to God.

My son Tyler told me that he will only marry a young lady if she is willing to go anywhere in the world God might lead them. She doesn't have to be called to be a missionary in the remotest parts of the globe, but she needs to be willing to go if and when God calls them. Tyler is positioning himself (and his future family) to say yes to God.

When Tyler met Emilie, he sensed she might be "the one." One evening he told me, "Dad, I'm having the big talk with Emilie tonight." I wondered what "the big talk was." He saw the puzzled expression on my face, so he explained, "Tonight I find out if she is willing to go to the mission field if God says 'go.'"

I appreciate Tyler's vision for a marriage and a family that is "full on and full out" for God. It's a firm foundation for a strong home.

AVOID DEBT

Debt is the enemy of immediate obedience. I can't tell you how many people have told me they can't do what God wants them to do because they've made financial decisions that seemed completely reasonable at the time but have shackled them to years of payments.

Early in our marriage, Cindy and I made a commitment to live in a way that we could walk away from our current position—wherever we were and whatever we were doing, no matter how old our kids were—in sixty days. That meant that we were forced to hold positions and possessions loosely, not clinging to them or cherishing them above God's spontaneous calling. If God told me today that He wanted me to move to Egypt or Argentina or Memphis, we could liquidate everything within two months and be there ready to serve Him with all our hearts. I don't ever want to be in a position to say, "God, I hear You. I'd like to obey You, but . . ."

"Spending creep" is rampant in our culture—and in our churches. Advertising is incredibly effective. The vast majority of us truly believe that we can't be whole and healthy people if we don't have the latest generation of technology and the next rung up the ladder of cars, houses, clothes, haircuts, restaurants, and everything else that's promoted—which includes an unimaginably long list! When we live in this way, we never have enough money because we spend every dime (or more) on the next thing.

I often tell young people (and older ones, too) to follow a simple financial principle: obey, pay, and delay. *Obey* God by tithing (or giving more than the tithe), *pay* cash for everything so you never borrow, and *delay* gratification so you're not always living at the edge or beyond your means. The decision to delay can't be made at the point of sale. It has to be a conscious choice made long before the decision of whether or not to buy.

To combat spending creep, Cindy and I decided to live a year behind our income. Actually, I've been delaying the next level of spending since I was twelve years old. It works like this: If you get a raise from $30,000 a year to $33,000, give ten percent of the raise ($300) and put the other $2,700 in savings. The next year, give yourself the raise of $2,700 and bank whatever new increase you get that year. This way, you always have enough money in the bank to say yes to God. People may think having only two or three thousand dollars in savings isn't much, but it's a ton of money compared to being broke!

Sometimes I talk to young couples getting by as the husband works while his wife finishes college. I suggest they use the delay principle with her entire salary after she graduates and gets a job: give ten percent of it to the Lord, and put the rest in the bank. It gives them the opportunity to make a sizeable down payment for a house or answer the Lord's voice in countless ways.

Finding creative ways to save and grow money is almost endless. When Tyler and Parker were young, we gave them the option of having big birthday parties or having smaller celebrations and putting the money we saved into an investment account for their future. That's what we've done for many years. It's amazing how much a little money can grow over time! The available money opens a world of possibilities for them. Not long ago, Tyler looked at the balance in the account and said, "Dad, I love the fact that I can say yes to whatever God calls me to do!" I love it, too. As he looks back, he isn't the least bit upset that he missed big, blowout birthday parties. He said, "There's no way I would trade this freedom and opportunity for better parties when I was a kid. No way!"

ELIMINATE DEBT

Many people haven't taken steps to avoid debt. For them, the pressures and limitations of owing money are a constant reality. The strain can be mentally and emotionally consuming. The nagging worry of being able to make the next payment colors every waking moment and every relationship. Counselors observe that couples have conflict over four main issues: children, in-laws, sex, and money, but the number one factor that leads to divorce is conflict over finances.[19]

A recent government report shows that the average debt in America is over $40,000 for every person with a credit report. In some states, the level is somewhat lower, but it's approaching $70,000 per person in California. The delinquency rate for credit cards and student loans is at or slightly above ten percent.[20]

These aren't just numbers. The figures represent values, heartaches, disputes, worries, and despair. Some people assume that if they can make the minimum payments on their credit cards they're in good shape. Far from it. If you owe $5,000 and make a minimum payment of $200 for five years at 18.9 percent interest, you pay a total $8,109—and that's assuming you don't make any additional purchases over those five years.[21] And for some, the interest rate is much higher, so they pay far more during that time.

When I talk about the problems associated with existing debt, people readily acknowledge how owing money complicates their relationships and clouds their thoughts. But some have told me, "You know, I don't think debt affects my spiritual life that much. God doesn't seem to be saying anything to me about money . . . or anything else, for that matter." I think their analysis is flawed. Indeed, God may not be speaking to them about any open doors to advance His kingdom because they aren't in a position to respond, but the problem may not be that God is silent. Perhaps the demands of the lenders and the constant mental fixation of making the next payment have plugged the person's spiritual ears.

Several very good and popular programs are available to provide guidance about getting out from under the weight of debt. Any of them will work if people have the discipline, tenacity, and vision to keep at them. There is always a price to pay for eliminating debt. You have to do one simple thing: live on less than you make so you can use the rest to pay down what is owed. The greater the difference between what you make and what you live on, the more you can pay the creditors and the quicker you can get out of debt. It's very simple, but it requires planning and discipline.

All of us, not just those who are financially drowning, are wise to delay upgrades. I drove a 1988 Honda Civic for the whole decade of the 90s. Could I have afforded a better car? Sure, but I valued the money I saved over the convenience of having a newer car. I banked the money I could have used for car payments all those years. When it was time to get a new one, I had more than enough.

I'm not saying it's wrong to have a new car or a comfortable house or fine clothes or anything else. I'm saying your first priority is to align your life with God. Everything else is far down the list. When anything or anyone else takes His place, you pay a much higher price than you can imagine because you aren't able to be sensitive and responsive to the voice of God. Eliminating debt brings freedom to do what God whispers for you to do.

I'm not saying it's wrong to have a new car or a comfortable house or fine clothes or anything else. I'm saying your first priority is to align your life with God.

HOLD POSSESSIONS LOOSELY

Christ is the King who rules over all, the Savior who paid for my sins, and the Creator who made it all. If I have even a glimpse of His greatness and grace, I realize everything I have comes from His hand. I don't own anything. I'm just a steward of the things He has given me for a short time while I live and breathe.

Those are high and noble thoughts, but how do we know if something has too much of a hold on our hearts? It's not hard to tell. What is it that you would have difficulty parting with if God said, "Give that." Many of us already can answer that question because God has been tugging on us for a long time. He knows which created things have taken the Creator's place in our hearts. In His love, He has asked us to give those things up so that He retains first place in our souls. It may be a deer rifle, a dining room table, a ring, a Corvette, or almost anything we can imagine. But it's not everything; it's *that* thing we don't want to give up.

A few years ago our church took up an offering for a ministry that helps young women escape human trafficking. When we looked in the collection plates, I saw an engagement ring. I knew it was Eunice Ferguson's. After the service, I asked her about it. She smiled, "That ring meant the world to me. For a long time, my husband couldn't afford to get me a ring. It was my dream, and I treasured it. Tonight, I sensed God speak to me and tell me to give it to help those girls."

Raymond is a young man who learned to hold things loosely. He sent me this note:

Pastor Rod,

At the beginning of this year you preached on "immediate obedience" when God speaks to us. The lesson really hit me. It was a new year, and I wanted to start it off right. The problem was I was still ignoring God's voice when it came to obedience. If I felt God telling me to give money in an offering, I did. I also gave time and money to others who asked me to help, and I trusted God in other areas of my life. The one area where I wasn't listening to Him was my possessions. The entire time you were preaching, the Holy Spirit was telling me, "Give up your Xbox."

At first I thought it was a guilty conscience for gaming more than I should, but I realized that wasn't the message. It was clear, but week after week and month after month, I ignored it. This summer I had the worst experience at work, and other events this year were equally as bad. I couldn't figure out why. I went to church

*regularly, tithed, worshiped, and did everything a "good Christian"
is supposed to do.*

*This weekend I had a breakdown. I felt overwhelmed by the
struggles in my life, but I knew what I needed to do. I needed to
spend more time with God—not just at church, but in my own
time. And I knew the reason I couldn't was because I was making
more time for pleasure than God. Enjoying my Xbox may not seem
like a big deal to others, but it is to me. It's the way I cope with stress
and loneliness, and it's how I define myself. I realized I couldn't
keep worshiping a box, because essentially, that's what I was doing.*

*So . . . I brought my Xbox to the church today to donate to
someone who will use it the way it's supposed to be used—as something to have fun with and not something to be worshiped.*

Raymond

START SMALL

When we read stories of people in the Bible or in church history
who demonstrated great faith, we marvel at their courage at a pivotal
moment. If we had the privilege of spending time with them prior to
that event, however, we would see a habit of obedience developed over
a long period of time. We don't need to wait for "the big moment" to be
obedient to God. We should start right where we are and do what we
know God wants us to do. For instance:

- Get up and go to church on Sunday morning (or whenever services are held).

- Sing instead of standing there like a knot on a log.
- Speak a word of kindness to a lonely person.
- Speak a word of kindness to an annoying person.
- Speak up when you know you should.
- Shut up when you know you should.
- Tell the truth with grace.
- Evaluate, but don't condemn.
- Don't believe a liar.
- Find a trustworthy friend.
- Forgive the person who hurt you.
- Open the door for an elderly person.
- Get up a few minutes early to read the Bible and pray.
- Give 10 percent of your income.
- Stop that bad habit.
- Respect the authority over you even if you disagree.

The list is endless, but God will show you plenty of choices you can make to obey Him right here and right now. The more responsive you are to the small things, the more open you will be to hear Him for bigger things.

When Jesus first met Peter after a long night of fishing and hauling in empty nets, He told him, "Put out into deep water, and let down the nets for a catch" (Luke 5:4). Jesus didn't lead off with, "Reach the world with the gospel," or "Prepare to die for Me!" He gave Peter a simple instruction. The fisherman offered an objection, but he decided to obey. Peter's response to Jesus was the beginning of an adventure of following Him.

As we take those small steps, we experience the joy of forging a real relationship with the God of glory. We realize He's always got our backs, and we see Him change lives—including ours. The more we obey, the more we align with God and the more we want to be even more closely aligned with His purposes.

> The more we obey, the more we align with God and the more we want to be even more closely aligned with His purposes.

Let me make the same point in reverse: if you aren't willing to be obedient to God in little things, you won't obey Him when He asks for something huge. Once a man proudly announced to me that he intended to give a million dollars to missions. I wasn't impressed for two reasons: First, he was calling attention to himself instead of God by his proclamation, and second, he wasn't already tithing his current income. When he told me, "One day, Pastor, I'm going to give you a million dollar check," I replied, "It won't happen until you give a hundred dollar check." He looked surprised, but he didn't write the check for $100. Maybe he planned to win the lottery or to invent the next generation of cell phone technology. I don't think God is impressed with grand pronouncements of our intentions if we aren't obeying Him in the little things in our daily lives.

The amount of money isn't the issue. God owns the cattle on a thousand hills. He doesn't need our money to accomplish His will. But He cares about love, loyalty, and obedience, and He gives us the unspeakable privilege of joining Him in seeing miracles of changed lives. If our hearts are in tune with His, we will be so generous with what we have that people will think we've lost our minds!

In our money, our time, and our relationships, we can get into alignment with God by obeying His clear instructions in the Scriptures. My money is His, my time is His, and every relationship is under His direction. Some people might conclude that this sounds narrow and suffocating, but it's just the opposite. It leads to freedom, joy, and thrills.

Pilots never take off without a flight plan, but upper level winds inevitably blow them off course. They have to be aware of their current location and the conditions so they can make a multitude of minor corrections to stay on course. In the same way, we need to be aware that the winds of our culture, the enemy of our souls, and our fallen human nature are always blowing. Like a pilot, we have to make corrections, too. Lamar Davis, Deputy Chief of Staff, Office of Governor Mike Beebe, is learning this lesson.

Pastor Loy,

Last year was an incredible time for me in terms of challenges and spiritual growth. Your focus on immediate obedience to God resonated with me. At times I found it easy to obey God completely, but at other times doubt, fear, and stubbornness prevented me from heeding God's direction.

Last November I tried focusing again on immediately obeying God. One afternoon I was returning to the capitol from lunch, and as usual, I took the exit closest to Children's Hospital. This is my normal route, but that day would be very different. As I exited off the ramp, I saw a person sitting on the rail of the overpass. I initially thought it was a worker, but as I got closer, I saw that it was a person in plain clothes sitting in the "jump position." I was shocked that nobody was there to help. I must admit that my first inclination was to drive by, and in fact, that's what I did. I came up with numerous reasons why I shouldn't get involved. Then I heard the Holy Spirit like never before saying, "You're here. Do something!" I decided to obey. I made a U-turn on the bridge and pulled over.

I got out of my car and saw it was a woman on the rail. I walked toward her and said, "Please let me help you. Let's talk about this." She replied that she didn't want to live, and then she began to cry.

As I got closer, I noticed an EMT running down from Children's Hospital. Together we approached her. When we grabbed her arms, she let go and began to fall. We tried to pull her up, but kept losing our grip. At that point a third man ran to us and reached over the railing to grab the lady's leg. The three of us pulled her up. By that time other EMTs had arrived to care for her. I got back in my car and left for work. I was shaken by the incident.

About a month later, I had become lax in immediate obedience. Instead of listening to God, I was more focused on fighting my ex-wife regarding visitation and work. When I realized my focus had slipped from God to my own problems, I realized I wasn't obeying God. In fact, I wasn't even listening for Him. I was filled with regret. The song "Say Jesus" was playing in my car, and I began to sing along and just call His name. The Spirit spoke to me so plainly and said, "Why don't you just surrender and say yes?"

It was as if someone was sitting in the passenger's seat. I began to cry. God assured me, and before I could formulate excuses or justifications, I began to say, "Yes, Jesus." I asked what He wanted me to do, and the Holy Spirit said, "Spread My Word to all people." I said "yes."

And now, Pastor, this is where I need you. I have accepted God's call on my life to spread His word, but I don't know what to do next. Will you help me?

Lamar

NEVER SAY NO

Every time we say no to God, we experience defeat at the hands of the enemy. When we say no, we miss God's will and His blessings. When we shake our heads and walk away, we're saying, "God, you may be King, but I know better. I'm choosing a different way." Our refusal may be out of arrogance or fear, but the results are the same: we're going our own way. Even if we've made a mess of our lives, God graciously offers us an opportunity to come back and say yes to start the process of reclaiming His will and His ways in our broken lives.

My goal—and my hope for every person who reads this book—is to become aligned so closely with God that I never have to say no to Him for any reason at any time. I want to be so sensitive to His voice that I hear Him when He speaks, and I want to be so responsive that I obey whatever He tells me to do.

Of course, there are certain things I hope God never asks me to do, but I don't close the door and bolt it shut. When I realize I'm resistant,

I ask God to change my heart so I want what He wants more than anything else in this world. And if He leads me in a direction I don't want to go, I'll still say yes because I trust He has a higher purpose than I can imagine. I sometimes pray, "Lord, adjust my heart to want Your will. I'm not going to say no, but I need You to change my desires." It has happened before, and I'm sure it will happen again. I trust that He knows best.

> When I realize I'm resistant, I ask God to change my heart so I want what He wants more than anything else in this world.

What's on your "off limits" list? Being a missionary to Africa? Sharing the gospel with your boss? Forgiving your parents? Standing up to an abuser? Caring for a spouse or a parent with Alzheimer's? All of us have something. What's yours? Be honest with God and ask Him to give you a pliable heart.

Can you imagine a church or a family where people encourage each other to get into and stay in alignment with God's truth and desires?

- What if we celebrate when we hear people talk about hearing God's voice?

- What if we dive in to help when they tell us they're taking steps to obey what He told them to do?

- What if, whatever God asked, the answer was a corporate and hardy "Yes!"?

- And what if the members of a church or family were honest when they *aren't* aligned so they could receive encouragement and support?

That's what the body of Christ is about. It's how we grow, how we heal, and how we expand God's kingdom to those who are watching.

And they're watching.

To have the attitude of Jesus, who was humble and obedient to the point of death (Phil. 2:5f), we need to constantly and purposefully align our hearts with His and obey Him in the small things. Immediate obedience is never saying no to God. It's learning to live and love like Jesus.

After I asked people in our church to take the challenge of listening to God's voice and responding in obedience for a year, I got a flood of stories. I want to end the book with one from a little girl who really gets it.

Pastor Rod,

On September 5, 2011, I received some terrible news from my mother that my father had passed away from brain cancer. As an eleven-year-old girl, that was very hard for me, knowing that I wouldn't see him again until we're all in heaven one day. I knew he had been suffering for almost three years, but I just didn't think it was fair because we prayed so hard for a miracle and believed he would be healed!

After I received the news, I went to my room crying and just being mad at God. I was yelling:

Why God? Why didn't you heal him? He loved you! He trusted you! We all trusted you! Why didn't you heal him?

Then all of a sudden, through all the crying I felt a sense of peace. God spoke to my heart in a soft, calm voice. This is what He said to me:

"Why do you not trust Me, young child? Why do you think I have abandoned you because I have not healed your father? Who do you think created the heavens and the earth? Why do you not know that he is singing and dancing around My throne? He is completely healed. I haven't abandoned you, my child. I do not abandon any of My children. I hear every prayer and bring every blessing. I have given you everything, My child. He is safe and sound, and so are you."

I knew immediately it was God who spoke to me and gave me such comfort. Since that day, I have had such peace. It gave me a whole new perspective on God's healing.

I learned that when you feel all alone and abandoned to remember: God never leaves even one of His children behind, no matter how far gone they are.

My name is Rose and my father's name is Tony, but most importantly, my God's name is Jesus!

This happened almost two years ago, and I will never forget that night when I felt true peace. My dad died at age fifty. I am now thirteen, my brother is eleven, and my mom is over forty. We all love Jesus very deeply and pray that one day we can be with my dad in heaven so we can worship Jesus together.

Rose

CONSIDER THIS . . .

1. Describe the process (and the necessity) of alignment in aiming missiles, in driving a car, in couples making important choices, and in negotiating rules and limits with teenagers.

2. What are some decisions people may make early in life that propel or block their future options to obey God?

3. Why is it essential to align our hearts with God's? What happens to obedience when our hearts aren't tender and thankful?

4. What do you need to do to avoid or eliminate debt? Who can help you? When will you start?

5. What does it mean to "hold possessions loosely"? Is there anything God has whispered to you that you're holding too tightly? If so, what's your next step?

6. What are three "small things" you need to do in obedience to God?

7.   What are the three most important principles, concepts, or lessons
     you've learned from this book?

And now, I invite you to take the 90-Day Challenge.

THE 90-DAY CHALLENGE

I want to invite you to take the biggest, boldest challenge of your life—to ask God to make you sensitive to His voice, and then, to obey whatever He asks you to do. I can't guarantee that He will speak to you every day, or every other day, or at any particular interval. And I won't promise that He'll speak to you in dreams, visions, audible voices, or miracles. But I will make this assurance: If you listen, He will speak; if you ask, He will answer; if you obey, He will open doors of opportunity to trust Him even more.

As you take this challenge, open your heart to the possibility that maybe—just maybe—God is working in, around, and through you to accomplish something far bigger than you ever imagined . . . and He wants you to join Him.

Determine a time when you have at least twenty uninterrupted minutes each day. Most people can set their alarms and get up a little earlier. Moms with little children will need to be more creative . . . and more flexible. Don't just hope you can "find the time." If that's your attitude, you will quit within a week. Make an appointment with God each day, and keep it. If you miss one day, it's not the end of the world. If you miss several in a row, be honest with God about your underlying hopes and fears. He will meet you in your honesty, too.

I have suggested a passage of Scripture for each day with some reflection questions. The goal isn't to complete the reading and answers as quickly as possible. The purpose is to open your mind and heart to God. If He speaks to you as you read the passage, stop and listen.

The questions are the same each day—not because I couldn't think of anything else, but because these are designed to prompt you to think deeply, listen intently, and evaluate your previous responses to God. Let me introduce the format for each day:

- Begin with a prayer of commitment to listen to God's voice and obey Him. God is worthy of our love and loyalty, so this prayer invites God to speak to you and be your King today.

- Read the passage of Scripture for the day. I encourage you to read it two or three times to let it soak into your mind and heart. If you have time, read it in context. Examine the paragraphs before and after, the chapter, or even the entire book or letter. God speaks most often and most clearly through His Word. Each day, ask the Spirit of God to open your mind and heart to understand what He is saying to you. He loves to answer that prayer!

- What is God saying through the passage? What was the author trying to communicate to his audience? What is God saying to you today?

- Reflect on your response to God's voice yesterday (or during the last few days). Did you hear Him tell you to do anything? Did you obey Him? Did you delay? Did you disregard His whisper for some reason? If you obeyed, what happened? How did you feel after responding to His voice?

- Remember that we are thoroughly human, so we obey imperfectly. Have you resisted or misunderstood God's instructions recently? If so, explain why and how, and identify the consequences.

- Finally, entrust your heart, your mind, and your day to God's love and care.

If you're in a small group, consider using this challenge as your content for discussion when you meet. The conversation will be rich and rewarding. If you're not in a group, you may want to ask a friend to join you in the challenge and meet weekly to talk about how you're learning to hear and obey God.

At any point in the ninety days, I invite you to post your account of how God has spoken to you, how you responded, and how He used your obedience. We have created a Facebook page for people to post their stories. Go to facebook.com/immediateobedience. There, you'll find plenty of inspiring accounts from people who are taking the challenge, and you can inspire others, too.

If you post a comment on this site, remember, it's public! Anyone can read it. You may need to change your name and some details to keep it anonymous. We can still celebrate with you!

This book provides a small space for you to write each day. If you need more room, get a notebook so you can express yourself more fully.

I can make one guarantee: If you'll take this challenge, your life will never be the same, you'll never look back, and you'll enjoy the adventure of your life. You can count on it.

1   Pray: "God, I'll do what You tell me to do, I'll give what You tell me to give, and I'll go where You tell me to go. Even before you ask, my answer is, 'Yes, Lord!' I am listening, Lord . . ."

2   Read the passage. What is God saying to you through this passage of Scripture?

3   Is God telling you to obey Him in a specific way today? If so, how?

4   From yesterday (or the past week), what did you hear God tell you to do? How did you respond? How did you feel after you responded?

5   Have you experienced any resistance or misunderstanding of God's directions during the past twenty-four hours? If so, describe it.

6   Pray: Ask God for humility to hear Him and courage to follow Him today.

DAY 1   LUKE 5:1–11

DAY 2   LUKE 5:12–16

DAY 3   LUKE 6:43–49

DAY 4   LUKE 8:22–25

DAY 5   LUKE 9:18–27

1   Pray: "God, I'll do what You tell me to do, I'll give what You tell me to give, and I'll go where You tell me to go. Even before you ask, my answer is, 'Yes, Lord!' I am listening, Lord . . ."

2   Read the passage. What is God saying to you through this passage of Scripture?

3   Is God telling you to obey Him in a specific way today? If so, how?

4   From yesterday (or the past week), what did you hear God tell you to do? How did you respond? How did you feel after you responded?

5   Have you experienced any resistance or misunderstanding of God's directions during the past twenty-four hours? If so, describe it.

6   Pray: Ask God for humility to hear Him and courage to follow Him today.

DAY 6   LUKE 10:17–24

DAY 7   LUKE 13:22–30

DAY 8   DEUTERONOMY 6:1–12

DAY 9   DEUTERONOMY 11:13–15, 25–28

DAY 10   DEUTERONOMY 12:28

1   Pray: "God, I'll do what You tell me to do, I'll give what You tell me to give, and I'll go where You tell me to go. Even before you ask, my answer is, 'Yes, Lord!' I am listening, Lord . . ."

2   Read the passage. What is God saying to you through this passage of Scripture?

3   Is God telling you to obey Him in a specific way today? If so, how?

4   From yesterday (or the past week), what did you hear God tell you to do? How did you respond? How did you feel after you responded?

5   Have you experienced any resistance or misunderstanding of God's directions during the past twenty-four hours? If so, describe it.

6   Pray: Ask God for humility to hear Him and courage to follow Him today.

DAY 11   DEUTERONOMY 15:4–6

DAY 12   DEUTERONOMY 28:1–6, 15–19

DAY 13   DEUTERONOMY 30:1–4

DAY 14   DEUTERONOMY 31:6–8

DAY 15   LUKE 14:25–35

1   Pray: "God, I'll do what You tell me to do, I'll give what You tell me to give, and I'll go where You tell me to go. Even before you ask, my answer is, 'Yes, Lord!' I am listening, Lord . . ."

2   Read the passage. What is God saying to you through this passage of Scripture?

3   Is God telling you to obey Him in a specific way today? If so, how?

4   From yesterday (or the past week), what did you hear God tell you to do? How did you respond? How did you feel after you responded?

5   Have you experienced any resistance or misunderstanding of God's directions during the past twenty-four hours? If so, describe it.

6   Pray: Ask God for humility to hear Him and courage to follow Him today.

DAY 16   LUKE 18:1–8

DAY 17   LUKE 18:9–14

DAY 18   LUKE 19:1–10

DAY 19   LUKE 19:11–27

DAY 20   LUKE 22:24–30

1   Pray: "God, I'll do what You tell me to do, I'll give what You tell me to give, and I'll go where You tell me to go. Even before you ask, my answer is, 'Yes, Lord!' I am listening, Lord . . ."

2   Read the passage. What is God saying to you through this passage of Scripture?

3   Is God telling you to obey Him in a specific way today? If so, how?

4   From yesterday (or the past week), what did you hear God tell you to do? How did you respond? How did you feel after you responded?

5   Have you experienced any resistance or misunderstanding of God's directions during the past twenty-four hours? If so, describe it.

6   Pray: Ask God for humility to hear Him and courage to follow Him today.

DAY 21   LUKE 24:36–49

DAY 22   JEREMIAH 7:21–29

DAY 23   JEREMIAH 9:23–24

DAY 24   JEREMIAH 11:1–5

DAY 25   JEREMIAH 29:11–14

1   Pray: "God, I'll do what You tell me to do, I'll give what You tell me to give, and I'll go where You tell me to go. Even before you ask, my answer is, 'Yes, Lord!' I am listening, Lord . . ."

2   Read the passage. What is God saying to you through this passage of Scripture?

3   Is God telling you to obey Him in a specific way today? If so, how?

4   From yesterday (or the past week), what did you hear God tell you to do? How did you respond? How did you feel after you responded?

5   Have you experienced any resistance or misunderstanding of God's directions during the past twenty-four hours? If so, describe it.

6   Pray: Ask God for humility to hear Him and courage to follow Him today.

DAY 26   JEREMIAH 31:31–34

DAY 27   JEREMIAH 40:1–3

DAY 28   JEREMIAH 42:4–6

DAY 29   PHILIPPIANS 1:3–11

DAY 30   PHILIPPIANS 1:27–30

1   Pray: "God, I'll do what You tell me to do, I'll give what You tell me to give, and I'll go where You tell me to go. Even before you ask, my answer is, 'Yes, Lord!' I am listening, Lord . . ."

2   Read the passage. What is God saying to you through this passage of Scripture?

3   Is God telling you to obey Him in a specific way today? If so, how?

4   From yesterday (or the past week), what did you hear God tell you to do? How did you respond? How did you feel after you responded?

5   Have you experienced any resistance or misunderstanding of God's directions during the past twenty-four hours? If so, describe it.

6   Pray: Ask God for humility to hear Him and courage to follow Him today.

DAY 31   PHILIPPIANS 2:1–11

DAY 32   PHILIPPIANS 2:12–18

DAY 33   PHILIPPIANS 3:1–11

DAY 34   PHILIPPIANS 3:12–21

DAY 35   PHILIPPIANS 4:4–9

1   Pray: "God, I'll do what You tell me to do, I'll give what You tell me to give, and I'll go where You tell me to go. Even before you ask, my answer is, 'Yes, Lord!' I am listening, Lord . . ."

2   Read the passage. What is God saying to you through this passage of Scripture?

3   Is God telling you to obey Him in a specific way today? If so, how?

4   From yesterday (or the past week), what did you hear God tell you to do? How did you respond? How did you feel after you responded?

5   Have you experienced any resistance or misunderstanding of God's directions during the past twenty-four hours? If so, describe it.

6   Pray: Ask God for humility to hear Him and courage to follow Him today.

DAY 36   ISAIAH 1:18–20

DAY 37   ISAIAH 40:27–31

DAY 38   ISAIAH 42:24–25

DAY 39   DANIEL 3:13–30

DAY 40   DANIEL 6:1–28

1 Pray: "God, I'll do what You tell me to do, I'll give what You tell me to give, and I'll go where You tell me to go. Even before you ask, my answer is, 'Yes, Lord!' I am listening, Lord . . ."

2 Read the passage. What is God saying to you through this passage of Scripture?

3 Is God telling you to obey Him in a specific way today? If so, how?

4 From yesterday (or the past week), what did you hear God tell you to do? How did you respond? How did you feel after you responded?

5 Have you experienced any resistance or misunderstanding of God's directions during the past twenty-four hours? If so, describe it.

6 Pray: Ask God for humility to hear Him and courage to follow Him today.

DAY 41   DANIEL 9:12–16

DAY 42   HOSEA 6:1–3

DAY 43   JOHN 1:43–51

DAY 44   JOHN 4:1–42

DAY 45   JOHN 7:37–39

1   Pray: "God, I'll do what You tell me to do, I'll give what You tell me to give, and I'll go where You tell me to go. Even before you ask, my answer is, 'Yes, Lord!' I am listening, Lord . . ."

2   Read the passage. What is God saying to you through this passage of Scripture?

3   Is God telling you to obey Him in a specific way today? If so, how?

4   From yesterday (or the past week), what did you hear God tell you to do? How did you respond? How did you feel after you responded?

5   Have you experienced any resistance or misunderstanding of God's directions during the past twenty-four hours? If so, describe it.

6   Pray: Ask God for humility to hear Him and courage to follow Him today.

DAY 46   JOHN 14:15–17, 23–24

DAY 47   JOHN 15:9–12

DAY 48   JOHN 16:5–16

DAY 49   JOHN 21:1–25

DAY 50   PSALM 1:1–6

1   Pray: "God, I'll do what You tell me to do, I'll give what You tell me to give, and I'll go where You tell me to go. Even before you ask, my answer is, 'Yes, Lord!' I am listening, Lord . . ."

2   Read the passage. What is God saying to you through this passage of Scripture?

3   Is God telling you to obey Him in a specific way today? If so, how?

4   From yesterday (or the past week), what did you hear God tell you to do? How did you respond? How did you feel after you responded?

5   Have you experienced any resistance or misunderstanding of God's directions during the past twenty-four hours? If so, describe it.

6   Pray: Ask God for humility to hear Him and courage to follow Him today.

DAY 51   PSALM 19:1–14

DAY 52   PSALM 51:1–12

DAY 53   PSALM 62:1–12

DAY 54   PSALM 63:1–11

DAY 55   PSALM 73:21–28

1   Pray: "God, I'll do what You tell me to do, I'll give what You tell me to give, and I'll go where You tell me to go. Even before you ask, my answer is, 'Yes, Lord!' I am listening, Lord . . ."

2   Read the passage. What is God saying to you through this passage of Scripture?

3   Is God telling you to obey Him in a specific way today? If so, how?

4   From yesterday (or the past week), what did you hear God tell you to do? How did you respond? How did you feel after you responded?

5   Have you experienced any resistance or misunderstanding of God's directions during the past twenty-four hours? If so, describe it.

6   Pray: Ask God for humility to hear Him and courage to follow Him today.

DAY 56   PSALM 83:1–4

DAY 57   EPHESIANS 1:3–14

DAY 58   EPHESIANS 2:1–10

DAY 59   EPHESIANS 4:1–6

DAY 60   EPHESIANS 4:20–32

1   Pray: "God, I'll do what You tell me to do, I'll give what You tell me to give, and I'll go where You tell me to go. Even before you ask, my answer is, 'Yes, Lord!' I am listening, Lord . . ."

2   Read the passage. What is God saying to you through this passage of Scripture?

3   Is God telling you to obey Him in a specific way today? If so, how?

4   From yesterday (or the past week), what did you hear God tell you to do? How did you respond? How did you feel after you responded?

5   Have you experienced any resistance or misunderstanding of God's directions during the past twenty-four hours? If so, describe it.

6   Pray: Ask God for humility to hear Him and courage to follow Him today.

DAY 61   EPHESIANS 5:1–13

DAY 62   EPHESIANS 5:21–33

DAY 63   EPHESIANS 6:10–20

DAY 64   PROVERBS 3:5–10

DAY 65   PROVERBS 10:20–25

1   Pray: "God, I'll do what You tell me to do, I'll give what You tell me to give, and I'll go where You tell me to go. Even before you ask, my answer is, 'Yes, Lord!' I am listening, Lord . . ."

2   Read the passage. What is God saying to you through this passage of Scripture?

3   Is God telling you to obey Him in a specific way today? If so, how?

4   From yesterday (or the past week), what did you hear God tell you to do? How did you respond? How did you feel after you responded?

5   Have you experienced any resistance or misunderstanding of God's directions during the past twenty-four hours? If so, describe it.

6   Pray: Ask God for humility to hear Him and courage to follow Him today.

DAY 66   PROVERBS 11:16–17

DAY 67   PROVERBS 13:2–6

DAY 68   PROVERBS 13:20–21

DAY 69   PROVERBS 14:16–18

DAY 70   PROVERBS 15:1–4

1   Pray: "God, I'll do what You tell me to do, I'll give what You tell me to give, and I'll go where You tell me to go. Even before you ask, my answer is, 'Yes, Lord!' I am listening, Lord . . ."

2   Read the passage. What is God saying to you through this passage of Scripture?

3   Is God telling you to obey Him in a specific way today? If so, how?

4   From yesterday (or the past week), what did you hear God tell you to do? How did you respond? How did you feel after you responded?

5   Have you experienced any resistance or misunderstanding of God's directions during the past twenty-four hours? If so, describe it.

6   Pray: Ask God for humility to hear Him and courage to follow Him today.

DAY 71   1 JOHN 1:5–10

DAY 72   1 JOHN 2:3–6

DAY 73   1 JOHN 2:15–17

DAY 74   1 JOHN 3:1–3

DAY 75   1 JOHN 4:7–12

1   Pray: "God, I'll do what You tell me to do, I'll give what You tell me to give, and I'll go where You tell me to go. Even before you ask, my answer is, 'Yes, Lord!' I am listening, Lord . . ."

2   Read the passage. What is God saying to you through this passage of Scripture?

3   Is God telling you to obey Him in a specific way today? If so, how?

4   From yesterday (or the past week), what did you hear God tell you to do? How did you respond? How did you feel after you responded?

5   Have you experienced any resistance or misunderstanding of God's directions during the past twenty-four hours? If so, describe it.

6   Pray: Ask God for humility to hear Him and courage to follow Him today.

DAY 76   1 JOHN 4:16–20

DAY 77   1 JOHN 5:1–5

DAY 78   ROMANS 2:12–15

DAY 79   ROMANS 3:21–31

DAY 80   ROMANS 6:15–18

1   Pray: "God, I'll do what You tell me to do, I'll give what You tell me to give, and I'll go where You tell me to go. Even before you ask, my answer is, 'Yes, Lord!' I am listening, Lord . . ."

2   Read the passage. What is God saying to you through this passage of Scripture?

3   Is God telling you to obey Him in a specific way today? If so, how?

4   From yesterday (or the past week), what did you hear God tell you to do? How did you respond? How did you feel after you responded?

5   Have you experienced any resistance or misunderstanding of God's directions during the past twenty-four hours? If so, describe it.

6   Pray: Ask God for humility to hear Him and courage to follow Him today.

DAY 81   ROMANS 8:1–17

DAY 82   ROMANS 8:28–39

DAY 83   ROMANS 12:1–3

DAY 84   ROMANS 16:19

DAY 85   1 CORINTHIANS 6:12–20

1   Pray: "God, I'll do what You tell me to do, I'll give what You tell me to give, and I'll go where You tell me to go. Even before you ask, my answer is, 'Yes, Lord!' I am listening, Lord . . ."

2   Read the passage. What is God saying to you through this passage of Scripture?

3   Is God telling you to obey Him in a specific way today? If so, how?

4   From yesterday (or the past week), what did you hear God tell you to do? How did you respond? How did you feel after you responded?

5   Have you experienced any resistance or misunderstanding of God's directions during the past twenty-four hours? If so, describe it.

6   Pray: Ask God for humility to hear Him and courage to follow Him today.

DAY 86   1 CORINTHIANS 13:1–13

DAY 87   2 CORINTHIANS 4:5–12, 16–18

DAY 88   2 CORINTHIANS 5:14–15

DAY 89   2 CORINTHIANS 9:6–11

DAY 90   2 CORINTHIANS 12:7–10

After you have completed the 90-Day Challenge, answer these questions:

- How has the challenge shaped your view of God, your sensitivity to His voice, and your desire to obey Him?

- What are your plans to listen and respond in faith during the *next* ninety days . . . and for the rest of your life?

ENDNOTES

1 "I'll Go Where You Want Me to Go," Text: Mary Brown, 1856–1918, Music: Carrie E. Rounsefell, 1894.

2 Oswald Chambers, *My Utmost for His Highest* (Discovery House Publishers: Grand Rapids, 2006), 30.

3 G. K. Chesterton, *The Collected Works of G. K. Chesterton, Vol. 4* (Ignatius Press: San Francisco, 1987), 23.

4 "Messiah," George Frideric Handel, 1741.

5 "And Can It Be That I Should Gain," lyrics by Charles Wesley, 1738, music by Thomas Campbell, 1825.

6 "Why 100 Former Muslims Converted to Christianity," Melissa Stephan, *Christianity Today*, April 18, 2013, cited at www.christianitytoday.com/gleanings/2013/april/why-100-former-muslims-converted-to-christianity.html

7 Rodney Starks, *The Rise of Christianity* (HarperOne: New York, 1996), 7, 73–94.

8 Cited by Clyde S. Kilby in *The Christian World of C. S. Lewis* (Grand Rapids: Wm. B. Eerdmans Publishing Company, 1995), 68.

9 Tim Keller, *The Reason for God* (Dutton: New York, 2008), 162.

10 Cited by Philip Yancey, *Where Is God When It Hurts?* (Zondervan: Grand Rapids, 1990), 257.

11 Francis Chan, *Crazy Love* (David C. Cook: Colorado Springs, 2008), 133.

12 John Maxwell, *17 Irrefutable Laws of Teamwork* (Thomas Nelson Publishers: Nashville, 2001), 148–160.

13 C. S. Lewis, *Mere Christianity* (HarperOne: New York, 1951), 121–122.

14 Philip Yancey, *Reaching for the Invisible God* (Zondervan: Grand Rapids, 2000), 75.

15 For more information about personality disorders, go to *Psychology Today's* website and review the diagnoses and symptoms. www.psychologytoday.com/basics/personality-disorders, or review the *Diagnostic and Statistical Manual of Mental Disorders, Fifth Edition.*

16 Josephus, *Antiquities of the Jews*, 19.344.

17 J. Oswald Sanders, *Spiritual Leadership* (Moody Press, Chicago, 1967), 150.

18 David G. Benner, *Desiring God's Will: Aligning Our Hearts with the Heart of God* (InterVarsity Press: Downers Grove, 2005), 15.

19 Cited by numerous sources, including Scott and Bethany Palmer, *First Comes Love, Then Comes Money* (HarperCollins: New York, 2009), 200.

20 "Five facts about household debt in the United States," Neil Irwin, *The Washington Post*, August 15, 2013, www.washingtonpost.com/blogs/wonkblog/wp/2013/08/15/five-facts-about-household-debt-in-the-united-states/

21 "Why Making Minimum Payments Gets You Nowhere," Tim Parker, Investopedia, July 12, 2012, www.investopedia.com/financial-edge/0712/why-making-minimum-payments-gets-you-nowhere.aspx

USING *IMMEDIATE OBEDIENCE* IN GROUPS AND CLASSES

This book is designed for individual study, small groups, and classes. The best way to absorb and apply these principles is for each person to individually study and answer the questions at the end of each chapter then to discuss them in either a class or a group environment.

Each chapter's questions are designed to promote reflection, application, and discussion. Order enough copies of the book for everyone to have a copy. For couples, encourage both to have their own book so they can record their individual reflections.

A recommended schedule for a small group or class might be:

WEEK 1: Introduce the material. As a group leader, tell your story of finding and fulfilling God's dream, share your hopes for the group, and provide books for each person. Encourage people to read the assigned chapter each week and answer the questions.

WEEKS 2–9: Each week, introduce the topic for the week and share a story of how God has used the principles in your life. In small groups, lead people through a discussion of the questions at the end of the chapter. In classes, teach the principles in each chapter, use personal illustrations, and invite discussion.

PERSONALIZE EACH LESSON

Don't feel pressured to cover every question in your group discussions. Pick out three or four that had the biggest impact on you, and focus on those, or ask people in the group to share their responses to the questions that meant the most to them that week.

Make sure you personalize the principles and applications. At least once in each group meeting, add your own story to illustrate a particular point.

Make the Scriptures come alive. Far too often, we read the Bible like it's a phone book, with little or no emotion. Paint a vivid picture for people. Provide insights about the context of people's encounters with God, and help people in your class or group sense the emotions of specific people in each scene.

Focus on Application

The questions at the end of each chapter and your encouragement to group members to be authentic will help your group take big steps to apply the principles they're learning. Share how you are applying the principles in particular chapters each week, and encourage them to take steps of growth, too.

Three Types of Questions

If you have led groups for a few years, you already understand the importance of using open questions to stimulate discussion. Three types of questions are *limiting, leading,* and *open.* Many of the questions at the end of each day's lesson are open questions.

Limiting questions focus on an obvious answer, such as, "What does Jesus call himself in John 10:11?" These don't stimulate reflection or discussion. If you want to use questions like this, follow them with thought-provoking, open questions.

Leading questions require the listener to guess what the leader has in mind, such as, "Why did Jesus use the metaphor of a shepherd in John 10?" (He was probably alluding to a passage in Ezekiel, but many people don't know that.) The teacher who asks a leading question has a definite answer in mind. Instead of asking this kind of question, you should just teach the point and perhaps ask an open question about the point you have made.

Open questions usually don't have right or wrong answers. They stimulate thinking, and they are far less threatening because the person answering doesn't risk ridicule for being wrong. These questions often begin with "Why do you think . . .?" or "What are some reasons that . . .?" or "How would you have felt in that situation?"

Preparation

As you prepare to teach this material in a group or class, consider these steps:

Carefully and thoughtfully read the book. Make notes, highlight key sections, quotes, or stories, and complete the reflection section at the end of each day's chapter. This will familiarize you with the entire scope of the content.

As you prepare for each week's class or group, read the corresponding chapter again and make additional notes.

Tailor the amount of content to the time allotted. You won't have time to cover all the questions, so pick the ones that are most pertinent.

Add your own stories to personalize the message and add impact.

Before and during your preparation, ask God to give you wisdom, clarity, and power. Trust Him to use your group to change people's lives.

Most people will get far more out of the group if they read the chapter and complete the reflection each week. Order books before the group or class begins or after the first week.

ABOUT THE AUTHOR

Rod Loy has been in full-time pastoral ministry for twenty-eight years. He is currently Senior Pastor at First Assembly of God in North Little Rock, Arkansas, a 102 year-old church. In the last thirteen years, under Rod's leadership, the church has grown to over 3,800 in average weekly attendance on six campuses.

His passion for missions has taken him to forty different countries. First Assembly gives over a million dollars to missions every year and has helped plant more than 1,100 churches in sixty-three nations.

He is the author of 3 *Questions: A Powerful Grid to Help You Live by the Grace of God.*

Rod's unique approach to leadership has led him to adventures in the "Real World," including working as a volunteer lifeguard at a water

park. A former children's pastor, Rod has helped develop the Faith Case curriculum for children and is still actively involved with kids. In fact, his office is in the preschool department!

He and his wife, Cindy, have been married for twenty-seven years and have two boys, Tyler and Parker. The whole family enjoys cheering for the Dallas Mavericks, four-wheeling, and the Arkansas Razorbacks.

The Loys live in North Little Rock, Arkansas.

For more information about First Assembly, ministry resources, or to watch services online, go to **firstnlr.com**.

Other resources by Rod Loy:

3 Questions: A Powerful Grid to Help You Live by the Grace of God

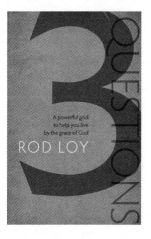

For more information about these books and many other resources,

visit www.influenceresources.com